POETRY now

THE STAGES OF LIFE

Edited by

Andrew Head

First published in Great Britain in 1998 by
POETRY NOW
1-2 Wainman Road, Woodston,
Peterborough, PE2 7BU
Telephone (01733) 230746
Fax (01733) 230751

HB ISBN 1 86188 692 6
SB ISBN 1 86188 687 X

FOREWORD

Although we are a nation of poetry writers we are accused of not reading poetry and not buying poetry books: after many years of listening to the incessant gripes of poetry publishers, I can only assume that the books they publish, in general, are books that most people do not want to read.

Poetry should not be obscure, introverted, and as cryptic as a crossword puzzle: it is the poet's duty to reach out and embrace the world.

The world owes the poet nothing and we should not be expected to dig and delve into a rambling discourse searching for some inner meaning.

The reason we write poetry (and almost all of us do) is because we want to communicate: an ideal; an idea; or a specific feeling. Poetry is as essential in communication, as a letter; a radio; a telephone, and the main criteria for selecting the poems in this anthology is very simple: they communicate.

'The Stages Of Life' is a wonderful collection of poetry written about subjects close to the heart. The anthology has a wide variety of poems which will either bring a tear to your eye or a chuckle to your throat.

The collection is written by the up and coming poets of today and is suitable for all ages.

The anthology expresses the joy and grief of *the stages of life*. Leaving home, starting a family and watching dear ones marry are all things we can relate to. These stages are expressed beautifully within this book.

CONTENTS

THE RAILWAYMAN

It was not a golden age of course;
There were those who found life
An insoluble problem. But childhood
Has its own vision, and ignorance
Remains a solid protecting cloak.

And so I came into this golden valley
Of summer and child-long days, drawn
Into a mysterious foreign land
By steam and Western Welsh:
Land of my grandfather, Ruler of
The Line, from Hay to Three Cocks
(Or somewhere thereabouts.)

He spoke softly, as if to allay fears
That his gigantic proportions might create.
He said little to me, that I can remember.
He was, after all, a man's man; not
An affectionate grandfather or father.
He talked and travelled with the real men,
And that was all right with me: he was
An illusion that I reached earnestly for,
But which shattered with the passing years.
He was simply a man of his time
And place, when we all needed heroes.

Roger Bradley

The Journey Of Life

The life long road begins at birth
A miracle makes up our worth
Into this world we're brought about
A special way no-one can doubt
The early stage of human life
Is unaware of any strife
Unaware of what's ahead
Just sleeps all day and then gets fed
The human then develops quick
No more nappies - no more sick
Instead it's pants, and time to walk
And pretty soon it's time to talk
Awareness now has reached its peak
Aware that now this life can speak
Aware enough to figure out
And find out just what life's about
From start of school to teenage years
The influence of fellow peers
The rights and wrongs that have been taught
Can result in feelings fraught
Yet soon this fraught is overcome
A lesson learnt 'What's done is done'
And gradually the years pass by
The answers come from questions 'Why?'
Growing old is the last stage
The book of life - the final page
The time to sit and contemplate
'Was the journey worth the wait?'

Lisa Smith

Seven Ages Of Man

When I peeped out of mummy's tum,
Me thought the end of the world had come.
Instead of my warm cosy place,
Was an ugly nurse with lighted face.
She was cold and dressed icy white,
She smacked my bot and squeezed me tight.
Free of her I began to crawl,
And with felt tip began to scrawl.
At school I learned to write much better,
I dropped blonde Heather, a sweet love letter.
At college, they made me chase funny ball,
With a point at both end, but no point at all!
At work, my bosses hated me like frantic,
Because I was brilliant and also romantic.
One day riding home on my trusty two wheeler,
I knocked over a filly and sent her a peeler.
Dismounting I asked if I could kiss her wound,
To my surprise the poor girl just swooned!
A week later we were married, to church organ's blast,
With Kathleen still covered with Elasto-plast,
No one taught us how, but we had three sons,
As I grew older they ate currant buns.
At sixty five I did retire, my poor wife she did perspire
And all the ladies me admire, to seduce me they did conspire.
Because they say I'm the plonker clone,
With seven ages, cocooned in one!

Peter N Lawrence

NANA

The flecks of powder settled in the seams of skin.
The lines have always been there,
But when did she change from fifty to ninety?

Twixt fifty to ninety they must have once been smooth.
Smooth and untroubled, like the pale and sparkling eyes
That watered my growth and shaped my habits.

Pale and sparkling eyes that watched her loved ones fade and leave her;
Leave her with the faith that they will meet again
And cradle her, as she once cradled me.

My world has never been without her;
And she will leave her comfort with me
In the tales she told and the dainty windowsill violets,
Touched by her and breathed on with her love.

But now she dozes in the autumn sun
In the garden I have made;
And waits for Winter's glory to claim her,
And cradle her, as once she cradled me.

Irene Baker

REBORN

Tiny fingers grasping
As into the world she emerges
Lungs filling with life
As her first breath she takes
Eyes focusing to the new surroundings she finds
Nostrils inhaling the scent of a new-being
Alien objects passed to her eager waiting mouth
Tongue tasting the formulated liquid inside
A feeling of security as she cuddles close to the warmth of the body
She will nurture, she will grow, into her own person
Into the reason she was put on this earth
And in years to come, the cycle will return again.

Ann Willbourne

I'm Old Now . . .

I'm old now,
But I remember when I was young,
Eagerly tackling every rung
I found upon the ladder of life,
Coping with zest with challenge or strife.

Youth passes too soon into middle age,
Another new chapter, a quieter stage,
Sometimes wondering whether and how
I'd feel when I'd say 'I'm old now!'

That day has come and I often yearn,
For the vigour of youth, and I wish I could turn
Around again the cycle of time
So that future and hope again were mine.
For love and life past with longing I burn,
Alas - I'm old now . . .

J O Coatswith

UNITED WE STAND

We never thought, when we got wed,
How would our life evolve?
We took everything for granted
No troubles to be solved.

How could we know through thirty years,
What problems there would be.
The pain, the tears, the happiness
We never could foresee,
But through it all, we stand here,
Survivors you and I,
Frayed around the edges,
But never asking why.
So, when life's finally done with us,
We'll take a cup of cheer,
To thank the lord for good times,
And be grateful we were here.

Linda Storer Smith

When a Child Leaves Home

I know that he loves me, and I'm sure he does care,
But I sit in my chair, and wonder about him.
What time will he be home tonight?
Will he be in before it is light?
Has he eaten today?
Are his clothes washed and dried?
Oh! How I've worried, oh! How I've cried!
For my child, now a young man,
Looking after himself as best as he can.

The life of a student, so full, and so busy,
When I think of it all, it makes me feel dizzy.
The late nights, the music, the homework all done!
A vast new experience and a whole lot of fun.

But life is so different for us now that he is gone.
His room is so empty, and there is no music on.
No clothes on the floor, no books on the bed,
No dent in the pillow, where he lay down his head.
No chaos, just order,
Everything in its place,
And we only have a photograph of his smiling face.

Gaynor Brownhill

THE LADS

A force to be reckoned with, the lads.
At any moment they would rattle the knocker
as they hurried past after the match,
committing their weekly act of love towards a mother who
sat in the kitchen, smoothing the green chenille table-cloth
or laying out cards for Patience.
A knock on her door would do it,
would remind her of the busyness of their lives,
tarmacing, bus driving, committee meetings at Anfield.
They were the lads, it didn't matter.
What did matter was that they called her Mam,
left their kids with her, sent birthday cards.

A lad can only do so much, after all.
At least she'd know they'd remembered her
as they dashed off to the Black Horse
to buy drinks for the most important members
who'd make the windiest speeches
in the parlours where their widows laid them out,
speeches about our names all being written down
in some big black book and Time waiting for no man.
(As if she didn't know that
as if she didn't know that
she could never, ever give her sons
what for years she'd had too much of.)

Shirley McDermott

Sonnet To Time Passing

Where did they go - those unforgiving years
That vanished in the twinkling of an eye?
Time that was filled with laughter and with tears
In almost equal measure, speeding by.
Where did Time go? - The minutes into hours,
Days, weeks, and months as seasons fled away,
Fresh Spring and glorious Summer's flowers,
Bright Autumn's tints and Winter's darker day.
Life gathers speed as year succeeds each year,
Our youthful strengths lost in relentless past,
Less able to resist the creeping fear
Of helplessness as we approach our last.
I'll shed no tears as I attain my end -
The grief is left for family and friend.

Joan Weston

The Small Room

In a very small room, long ago, far away,
Ecstatic lovers, forsaking of others,
Unshakeable trust, and faith in the Lord,
Gave themselves in love, and in time, I was born.

In that very small room with love's special right
Protected from harm in the red velvet night
For nine blissful months, the room was my own
Welcomed and nurtured my presence was formed.

In that very small room I moved and I swayed
Twisting and turning, pushing I made, but
Forceful contractions from outside the room
Thrust me downwards and outwards to a very big room.

I screamed and I cried, struggling in vain
Thinking, 'I'll never be pushed out again'
Noisy, blinding, jostled and torn, it
Made me wish, I had never been born.
The final discourtesy severed the cord:
I reached out for help, and there found the Lord.

I knew from that time, He would always be there
Though to my small room I could not repair, but
Sometimes in bed in the rage of a storm
I draw down deep like a foetus unborn, and
In the warm bedclothes despite the dark room,
I capture the comfort of my small room.

Lee Jenson

SUBJECT TO STATUS

He sat huddled in the
doorway of an empty
shop,
alone amid the babel of
the January sales;

A late teenager
with skin creased as
discarded cellophane;

Eyes watering,
pupils staring like
pebbles beneath the surface
of a frozen pool;

His heart broken,
his soul flooded,
eyelids unable to hold
back the weight of his
tears;

A casualty lost in the
nowhere land of his pain;
hands outstretched, palms up,
reaching deeply into the
indifference of passing
shoppers;

Above fidgeting starlings
and neon angels he stared,
dreaming of a warm bed and a
familiar hand reaching across
clean sheets.

Roger McDonald

DAYS GONE BY

With washing machines the common thing to get clothes clean, - no
need to scrub,
In days gone by, washday was spent scrubbing near the 'Dolly Tub';
Two Buckets and a Yoke were used to carry water from the spring,
A lot of rain was kept in barrels for washing clothes and everything.

The Wringer stood inside the Wash-house, near the door into the yard,
There were no Spinners to spin out water, just imagine - those
days were hard!
The clothes were dried out on the line, across the yard from
Pole to Pole,
Sometimes marked by little smuts of sooty smoke or dust from coal.

The Smoothing Iron was by the fire, it was tested with a drop of spit;
Fingers wet with some cold water was another way of testing it.
The Toilet was across the yard, a Bucket under a wooden seat,
The Council emptied it twice weekly, though it did not smell so sweet.

There were no Radios or Television to tell the scandal of the town,
Just a good old 'spicy' gossip, kept a person from feeling down.
Lighting was by Gas or Oil, giving the light to read or write,
So the evening passed quite quickly, early to bed nearly every night.

Because a Gas Stove was a luxury, the oven was heated by
Coal or Wood,
The Kettle was boiled on the Fire, which also cooked most of the Food.
There were no Fridges then, one took care to keep food good,
A cupboard made from Wood and Gauze, kept the Flies
from off the Food.

A Horse drawn cart brought Milk and Eggs, fresh Milk brought daily
was a treat,
The Baker called with Bread and Cakes, the local Butcher
delivered Meat.
The Grocers Boy delivered groceries, goods were brought in
many ways,
When we look back and think of it, were those really *'The good
old days?'*

F Brown

A Long Way

This mornings' mourning day
memorial of two world wars,
I awoke to sounds of singing.
'It's a long, long way to Tipperary.'
And I thought of those fading ghosts
of youthful men, their lives,
real and individual to each of them
as your life is to you,
mine to me,
marching in long, long lines . . .

Singing, singing, singing,
all the old songs
that linger poignantly
on the stale air
of this dwindling century.

Oh men,
your youth and strength exploited,
how faintly now your spirits
march through the swirling mists
of living memory
and soon you will move
like figments of imagination,
only across young minds
alongside the hazy heroes
of Hastings, Agincourt, Trafalgar
and all history book battles,
studied mainly as a part
of examination courses.

'It's a long, long way . . . '

M Munro Gibson

A Man, My Son

You're a man that I am proud of
A son who is loving and smart
Looking back to the days of your childhood
There's a special place in my heart
From your school days you made so much headway
Achieving and reaching your goals
Now you're heading in the right direction
My pride seemingly over flows
I have watched you grow up making your way
In a world where there's much to be found
For you studied and made an impression
From a boy now to manhood you're bound
Over years you gained knowledge and learning
You have reached for success in your life
With positive thoughts for a future you know
Will be challenging, varied and bright.

Jeanette Gaffney

One Morning Waking

One morning waking,
I grew up.
It seemed an ordinary day.

Nothing looked different
to what it was before,
but inside it was different.

That was the first time
it came to me
my mother would one day die.

I was afraid.
Even the flowers felt it,
it coloured my whole day.

I wasn't at all myself
the day I grew up.
My mother worried about me.

After that
I stayed grown up
till the day my mother died,

and on that morning,
waking,
I never felt so much a child.

Lily O'Sullivan

My Lifetime With Snow

When as a child and saw the snow I couldn't wait to play,
And eagerly looked forward to more lovely games next day.

And then I started infant school - snow still a great delight,
Looked forward to the weekend when I played from morn' till night.

At prep school we had snowball fights, our hands were red and raw,
We built a snowman on the lawn - it stayed there till the thaw.

Next stage I was at college and learned to skate on ice,
I also found that 'dating' was really rather nice.

Winter at University brought skiing on the slopes,
Then thinking of the future, and building up my hopes.

Next thing, I'm getting married - my bridal dress is white,
As is the snow which blocks the road on honeymoon that night.

The years go by, I've children now and they too love the snow,
They bring back happy memories of mine so long ago.

It's January - the days are cold - the nights are even colder,
Another bright new year begins - but I just feel much older.

So now I've gone full circle and all my ages done,
I do not like the snow so much - I just prefer the sun.

Brenda Dolley

Now And Then And When . . .

Never has the ascent
Of the moon
Looked so beautiful
As it has tonight
And I believe
Everything
Anyone has ever said
But only tonight
I'm amazed
I've survived tonight
But I have
And I'll be back
To see the end
I'll be back
Alive to see the end
Back
Alive
To see the end.

Kenneth Bavel

My First Born Child

My first born child
Is cute as can be
She has tiny feet and tiny toes
Tiny little fingers
That will grow.

Her hair is blonde and eyes of blue
She is growing up and
Now she is two.

Now she is growing faster
Into a teenager with spots
On her face she wears
Fashionable clothes that's a disgrace.

Now she is a woman
She will be going down the aisle
In style
She will also have
Her first born child.

Christine Noden

THE JOURNEY

When you are young, eternity's ahead,
Sixty years, seventy, or even more.
You can't believe one day you will be dead,
Like all the generations gone before.

Comes work, then marriage, as a man or wife.
In subtle stages Time has you beguiled,
Until you're in the middle rank of life,
Child to a parent, parent to a child.

You watch him grow, and then admit the truth
That he's outstripped you in his strength and speed;
Untiring, confident of endless youth,
While you must feel your energies recede.

Now look, and see that the front line has gone,
And while you mourn them, comes the revelation
That you must face the Enemy alone,
For you are now the older generation.

Old age is breaking you; it's seen you grow
Arthritic through the ravages of Time,
Stiff kneed, with aching back and footsteps slow,
The road too long, the hill too steep to climb.

You're ready now for what you feared before,
And soon your pain and weariness will end,
For God has opened wide for you a door,
With Death no longer Enemy, but Friend.

Reine Errington

Love

We are such dumb species,
put on this earth for what,
for pain, for love, for nothing,
surely someone knows the plot,
for love is not love,
just hurting again,
love and nothing mix,
which causes real pain,
love has no point,
just helps you through life,
but pain can be worse,
as sharp as a knife.

J Titchener

A HAIKU: THE SEVEN AGES OF MAN

Baby:	Baby whines and wails, Reaching for his mother's arms, Wanting food and love.
Schoolboy:	Off he goes to school! Thirsty for knowledge and facts, Always ready to learn.
Lover:	Forever besotted, He sings his loved one's praises. He's hers completely.
Soldier:	Full of promises, He's out to make his mark, Seeking reputation.
Justice:	Older and wiser, His opinions are guides, Earning him respect.
Pensioner:	Ageing fast and soon. Clothes too big for shrunken body; Old age has set in.
Senile:	Memory has gone, So has the mind, leaving nothing - Only a helpless body.

Lucy Woollard

The Stages Of Life

Night comes, and with its coming,
sleep chases all our cares away.
Dreams that take us to another period
till morning light brings forth the new born day.

So do the years too swiftly pass,
and we too grow apace in age,
moving from one scene to another,
actors on life's ever changing stage.

Schooldays that seemed so never ending,
the youthful years that followed after,
the joys and pains of young love and sorrow,
and days of fun, sweet hope, and laughter.

Comes middle age and all its worries,
with neither youth nor age to recompense
for times that now evade recapture,
and dreams to give way to common-sense.

So arrives old age, and with its coming
we travel down sweet memory's long lane,
and lingering, listen to its telling
of the times we treasured most and live again!

Mary Ward Hunt

The Outcast

At eighteen his problems really began,
When the home where he stayed sent him packing.
They said it was time he became a man,
He tried tempers and begging and pleading.
He did not want to leave, he made a fuss.
All they gave him was the fare for a bus.

With a weary heart he headed on out,
To try and find lodgings for the night.
But of rooms there were not many about,
And the cost was giving him quite a fright.
Experience in the world he did lack,
Another door slammed in his face with a whack!

No-one wants you when you don't have a home,
You're a waster and a drifter you see.
Now the lonely streets he would have to roam,
Begging for money for a cup of tea.
People ignored him, he was just a bum,
His only crime; he did not know his mum!

With rain running down the neck of his coat,
He was frozen and soaked through to the skin.
He was not feeling well his throat did croak,
Losing weight and exceedingly thin.
He needed help but nobody was there,
The caring society did not care.

A friend gave him something, to ease the pain,
Though he knew in his heart it was wrong.
He was never to be the same again,
But he was weak where once he was strong.
He was an outcast of the human race.
He was found in a box; death on his face.

Warren Galley

Cast Adrift In Life

Our eyes upon an ocean, see
joy, fulfilment, insanity.
Softly splashing waves caress
a shore of graves soon possessed.

Cast adrift in life we see
loss, anger, calamity.

Awashed and sodden
soaked and trodden
we twist and turn
in tides of fate.

Cast adrift in life we see
quietly pleasing harmony.

Helen Rodgers

AGE

The man and the tree grow old together
though separated by a hundred years their birth:
both are creviced and cracked,
he with lichened eyebrows and moss - tufted ears
betrays an exuberance of the unnecessary
as does the tree, misshapen, fungus - clad.

Together they are dying:
both have limbs more brittle now
as sluggish circulation of the blood and sap
stiffens branches, crooks arms and knees
and all their joints swell awkwardly and creak.

The storms will cause this bough to snap
and shake his fingers, legs; his steps will falter.
Nothing now can alter
this continuing process of gradual dying
despite the shared beauty won
of experience and endurance long in years.
Though now they're weak,
they'll stand till, when disease - attacked,
they fall at last
and both return to earth.

Beryl Turing

The Image

(For Florence)

I met mortality today,
His skin hung loose, his hair was grey,
He saw me in the mirror too,
And told me frankly, 'I am you!'

'Since Earth developed you were not.
For aeons hence you will not be,
But for the brief space in between,
This mirror image you can see.

You met me first when we were two,
We barely realised who was who,
My face reflected on the shelf,
Gave you a picture of yourself.

I watched you growing taller, stronger -
An adolescent, spending longer,
Inspecting what her eyes might see.
You weren't at all aware of me.

Then we met shaving every day,
Your manhood dawned and came to stay,
I saw you on the morn you wed,
And her reflection by the bed.

I watched your dark brown hair recede,
And pale to a distinguished grey,
As year by year the wrinkles came,
And youthful features fled away.

Ages had passed before you came.
Light years will pass when you are gone.
Will any then recall your name,
When all too soon, your days are done?

Though now you see me here today.
It's nearly time to go away,
For fate drives but in one direction
And life is but a brief reflection.'

Ron Ravenhall

VALETE

I see you now, in memory's eye,
As first-year students neat and spry,
Wide-eyed, expectant, poised and keen,
Attendant, punctual, spruce and clean.
I know you now with coiffure dyed,
With straggling beard and musk applied,
With down-cast eyes - excuses sighed
For work that's late or never tried.

I hear you now, in memory's ear,
As first-year students tinged with fear,
In talk discreet, in accents clear
From Ireland, Wales and places near.
I know you now that, in a flash,
You'll voice opinions firm and brash,
Seek out debate, embrace the clash,
Nor heed the lecturer's withering lash.

I struggle still, in memory's pit,
With book and board and laboured wit
To trace the logic of all of it
Revealed and told in Holy Writ.
I say no more. We've had our day.
(Oh! Wittgenstein: what games we play.)
Meaning and truth will still hold sway
Tho' justified in varied way.

I welcomed you in autumn mists,
Mere printed names on formal lists:
Three winters' snows our cheeks have kissed
And now in May the heart-strings twist.
I wish you well. Live out your dreams!
Life is much more that what it seems.
There's no truth in the things we see:
It's all a matter of necessity.

Raymond Holley

UPON THE DEATH OF A CHILD

(Dedicated to Rowan (1982 - 1997)

Speak not to me of sorrow,
Or of it 'being God's will'
Do not come grieving, quietly,
Or tread soft, or talk in whispers.
But share with me the rage,
The angry storm of indignation.
The rising scream of torment
As we form the question, 'Why?'

David Anderson

A New Beginning

God created men and supplied his every need
A plan so great and wonderful so selfless will succeed.

Man toiled and tilled the earth the power was in his hands
Against all hostile elements he cultivated lands.

Then the finding of earth's resources unexpectedly began
The age of ice, iron, stone, bronze, such wealth inspired man.

So far from God man wondered in his quest of greed and might,
He forgot a promise made to Abraham on that dark and starry night.

Joy, love and peace God now sent down to earth
This new life was manifest in Christ Jesus' Birth.

Discoveries and reformation the age of steel evolved
Now the age of space man's mind and intellect revolved.

So privileged are we as new millennium heirs the future again is in
our hands,
Can we strive to unite each body and soul, a true selfless inspired band.

Olive Bedford

FOOTSTEPS

One day we were commanded to fly.
We soared like eagles on the reckless sky,
And plummeted over the domains of the Earth,
Our minds free in our rebirth.

The man stands alone,
On the surface of a barren and lifeless moon.
The first to lay a footprint on the virgin dust -
He is the summit of human achievement.

He turns towards home, feeling utterly isolated.
Slowly, the crescent rises above the horizon -
A cobalt sapphire against the diamond stars.
The Earth brings the only colour to the man's eyes.

He takes a few steps,
And utters the words that will forever be remembered.
The signal is sent home to a planet of rejoicing people,
Who, for those few minutes, have no race, no borders.

The children of Earth have taken their first footsteps in to a wider realm.

July 20th 1969: 'That's one small step for man . . . One giant leap for mankind.'
Neil Armstrong - First man on the moon.

Sylvia Spence

Change Of Life

Sleep.
The last vestige of innocence.
With eyes closed the world of the man vanishes
and in silence, the dream,
the world of the boy flourishes.

A child censored from the heaviness of doyen
wakes in the dawn of another day.
He hears the song of the bird,
tastes the fresh air of this planet,
and wonders at the morning star.

The man wakes at the sound of his alarm clock.
Heedless of the spiral gyre he rushes,
deaf to the birds,
pollutes the air with his fumes
and is oblivious to the morning star,
invisible in its brilliance.

Simon P Conquest

TRANSITIONS (TO ADULTHOOD)

The innocence of youth
Mistakes, always an excuse
Neutralised by joy, fun
Optimism and laughter
Adult indulgence, remembered hereafter

Evolves into the 'Troublesome Teens'
Characterised by Moody Boys and 'Drama Queens'
Don't realise . . . it's rampant hormones,
Hidden hopes and fears
Which hopefully materialise
Or dissolve over the years

Next stage our 20's
Scene moves into 'Adult Territory'
Mysteries unfolding, sometimes maturity
Confidence rollercoaster - who is the driver?
Have to take the reins
Learn to be assertive and wiser

Moving on . . .
What age do we ever grow up?
Tell me, where do we go to 'Find ourselves'?
Fear of maturity might make you throw up
Evolution was never easy
Finding yourself might make you feel queasy

Emotional maturity for the good of all
My goal is to find the 'Real Me'
Someone our parents would be real proud of
With the proviso, 'I'm doing it for me'.

Eileen McCrory

Return From River Island

We who are dead but cannot rest,
Now return from River's Island.
And we journey,
All through the long night
Of silent tear, and moments
Of the morning mists,
To meet your screeching day.
And we come,
Urgent, upon the every ripple
Of the laboured oar,
In our ghost boats of great concern;
All through the blood swept reaches
Of the falling moon,
And the sunset clouds of dying light,
Into your world to say . . .
'What are you teaching your children now?
For we only see a barren land,
And emptiness hangs
On every missing tree,
And the mountains no longer move
To the sacred river's flow,
Without a clear sky to sing the song upon'
And would you listen if we said,
'That without care of mother earth,
Only the bitter root can form
Bearing the no fruit at all,
And so therefore
There can be . . . no rhyme.'

Norman Royal

Eyes

See through the eyes of a child,
See all that is meek and is mild,
See all that is coy and is joy, is happiness,
Games, is rhymes is time that goes too fast.

See through the eyes of youth,
See you seeking the truth
See the future a rose to be plucked,
By waiting and growing and learning and knowing
And the reaping and sowing of time.

See through eyes full grown,
See truth in learned things known
See all your illusions quietly die,
As you toil and you sorrow and you
Work and you borrow so there's money tomorrow
To keep the wolf from the door.

See through the eyes of the old,
Even the summer is cold,
Tired and weary and stiff with age,
Your passage through life has run out of rage,
The laughter, the tears, the hopes, the fears
Have drifted away in the mist of years,
And you smile,
As your eyes gently close.

Hamish Lee

THE AGES OF WOMAN

The world is bathed in cold vibrating light,
When the girl child is placed at her mother's breast.
The warmth and love, tears and strife,
Are yet to come for this little mite.

In April when thin branches bristle with spitting buds,
The girl child skips and learns and plays.
Snared raindrops quiver like jewels on the gate,
And the future is bright to the girl child's gaze.

In May when sweet blossoms scent the air,
She tastes the sweetness of lovers meeting.
By August when green globes of fruit nod in the warm air,
She is fulfilled, content, with mother Earth.

Come October, when leaves lay tattered at the foot of the trees,
Time has left faint colour on her cheeks.
Her bones are burnt into her body,
Showing to the world her passing years.

But December has its beauty too,
Each woman shares in this.
Her role in life to reproduce,
Has passed on to another.

And so she integrates with Earth,
And nature takes its course.
And spring will come again in time,
And prove to us her worth.

B Wildsmith

The Seven Ages Of Man

All the world's a screen
And all the men and women merely viewers
They have their heroes and their heroines
And one man in his time sees many parts
His acts being seven ages.

First the infant in his mother's arms
As yet unaware of the flickering images
Or what the future presages for him.

Then the schoolboy with his heavy bag of books
Hurrying after school to watch Blue Peter
And toying unwillingly with homework.

Then the young, but drug-emboldened lover
Scattering his profligate seed where he will
And abandoning his carelessly begotten progeny
To the DSS.

Next the terrorist, hoarding his semtex
And perpetuating his prejudices to the
Third and fourth generation
And beyond.

Then the barrister, complete with VDU
And the ubiquitous internet
Dispensing his expensive advice
And growing rich.

The sixth age shifts to the youngish pensioner
Studying his holiday brochures for yet
One more trip to foreign climes
Appreciative of the ready availability of spare parts
Hips, knees, corneas, kidneys and hearts etc.

Last scene of all, the hospice patient
Grateful for the soft ministering hands
Wafting him gently to other lands
Happy to die.

Doris Taylor

A Thought For Peace

What about the ruler when power takes his hand
Never quite contented with just his own land.
What about the people just like me and you
They're the ones with most to lose, and very often do.
What about the children, some have lost their mums
Their life will never be the same, they're the lonely ones.
What about the women left alone to cry
Thinking of the ones they love, why did they have to die.
What about the farmer his land is very small
But when the tanks go rolling by, he has no land at all.
What about the country, when all the tanks are still
They look around, they've had enough, there's no more blood to spill.
What about the children, let all the nations say
Give them time to all grow up, not just be blown away.

Evelyn Ingram

FIRST LESSON

We brought our daughter
to the edge of the school-yard.
There we straightened and dusted
through our parental litany,
our laying on of hands.
We kissed her
and let her go.

Moist-eyed, we watched
her stepping away into another world.
At our own edge and feeling abandoned
we held hands
communing softly through our fingers.

She looked so small.
Her Mickey Mouse school-bag
cartooned across her tiny shoulders
and her bright bloused arms
stuck out at funny angles;
her little bumps of knees and spindly legs
seemed suspended beneath her pinafore;
her sensible black shoes looked huge
while appearing to hardly touch the ground.

Yet, above all, her hair bounced happily free.
Without a backward glance she absorbed
the little group milling in the middle of the yard
then, almost as an afterthought,
tendered us a reassuring wave and turned
to swallow up the building.

Stephen Eric Smyth

7 Ages Of Man

Expelled from the peace of that special place
Harsh lights and strange noises ending the race
Man, as a baby, lets you know his dismay
And cries for the comfort he's lost on the way

Now clean and dry but with an angry unrest
Continues to cry till he's found her sweet breast
He suckles and sighs in blissful content
His will fulfilled at this happy event

Man as a child continues his quest
The spur is his need to make a success
He doesn't look back as he forges ahead
His aim, his ambition, by which he is led

Man as a youth is fired with desire
The world as his oyster he's keen to acquire
He won't recognise failure whatever he does
Every aim he achieves just adds to the buzz

Man, when at last the age of consent
Has raised his hopes and broadened his bent
His majority reached he looks for a wife
He needs a catalyst to enhance his life

Man in his prime has now reached his goal
Wife and children to make his life whole
But still he is searching and looking for more
To use up energy he's managed to store

Middle-aged man now stops to look back
He has had his life, nothing much is lack
And still he tries to keep up with the young
But finds in his aim he gets himself stung

At last, an old man now, his time running out
Memory going and he's grown rather stout
All he longs for is comfort and a loving wife
Who will comfort and nurse him the rest of his life

At last the flame has dimmed and expired
He has gone at last, no longer tired
Dust to dust, ashes to ashes, deep in the earth
No longer a subject of cruel banter and mirth.

Royston E Herbert

Youth

Fire and thunder
Peace and war
Pride and passion
Carnivore.

Blind rebellion
Brimming rage
Dark frustration
Awkward age

Understand him
Blatant youth
Needing freedom
Seeking truth.

Dreams, ambitions
Nature's plan
Is what you're made of
Nearly Man.

Bernadette Morris

Untitled

Opening the book of photographs, the
Hand caresses the faded sepia print,
A hint of yellowing round the edges
The innocent baby face looks up
Quizzically, the beginnings of a smile
For the man with the camera,
Large brown eyes like a seal,
Against a plumped-up purple cushion,
And the hand turns quietly over to
The next . . .
Schoolboy black, and bursting with
Questions, unsure of their framing but
Conscious only of the urgency of them,
Half-truths that taunt, and friends that
Flaunt their new-discovered bodies
For the bewildered.
Turn on, and to a marriage day,
Vibrant, bright and gay, the pride
Of bride in organdie and lace.
The photograph inside, of love that
Must abide, in this album it takes
Glowing, pride of place . . .
Some homely pictures now,
Of children in a row, the pride
Of father, mother, and the rest.
The lines around the face,
Now add a certain grace, although
The subject now may've past his best.

A few more pages on, last trace of youth
Has gone, the hand that turns the pages
Lingers now, and lastly in the book,
A pale exhausted look, the pulse of
Life is starting now to slow.
For with a gentle touch, and lovingly
As such, befits the one who caused the
Book to be, *He* sets the picture free.

Stephen Voyce

RECOLLECTION

I look through the window, the window of life,
And live yet again its trouble and strife.
I see yet again those that I once knew,
The friends that were many, the enemies few.
Schoolmates and shipmates, companions of youth,
Those that caused hurt and those that spoke truth.
Oft', when I'm lonely, I wish that I might,
Once more as they were then, hold them in my sight,
Sadly I know that many have died,
Yet must I put sadness and sorrow aside,
For they are alive, in my memories far-flung,
In glad recollection they'll always be young.
So, as I grow older, and not knowing where,
I hope when we meet, they will welcome me there.

David G Hood

SONG FOR CRAIG

He was lonely and unloved, often filled with bleak despair,
His family did not seem to want him, they did not seem to care,
He did have *some* good friends,
He knew they would be there.

He got in trouble with the police, he even went to jail,
Nobody to care, nobody was there,
To love him.

He even got a job, it did not last too long,
He keep on getting drunk, they could not keep him long.

One dark rainy night, in a mood of hopelessness and despair,
He got knocked over by a car,
Nobody was there, nobody to care.

He discharged himself from hospital, his life was pretty tough,
He would like to exit from this life,
He had really had enough.

His few and only good friends, begged him to go back,
It could be that he would die,
His family would not really care,
But, the tears his friends would cry.

Now, I do not really know Craig well,
But I care what happens to him,
Perhaps one day he will be well, then he will work again,
He will have a wife, children and a home,
He will have peace and stability,
He will not be alone, anymore.

Each night before I go to sleep, I say a little prayer,
Because I want God and Craig to know, that *someone* does really care,
I wish that I could wipe out, the pain of all his young years,
I hope that one day he will find peace,
And there will be *no more tears.*

Linda Kathleen Harker

THE AGES OF MAN

When I was a baby
Walking and talking
Was something the toddlers did
I was content
With eating and sleeping.

When I was a child
Kissing and smooching
Were things that the older ones did
I was content
With playing and learning.

When I was grown up
To get on in the world
Was something the middle-aged did
I was content
With courting and drinking.

When I was middle-aged
Becoming feeble and sick
Was something the elderly did
I was content
With getting and spending.

Now I am old myself
To die and be buried
Is something we all must do
I must be content
With sitting and waiting.

John A Davis

SANS SENSE?

Old Age comes galloping up on one.
Youth's here today, tomorrow gone.
Sans hair, sans sight, sans teeth they say -
Sans everything. Oh, lack-a-day!
The memory fails. Remember when . . . ?
Oh dear, oh dear, it's gone again.
Is that a ship far out at sea?
Again my eyes are failing me.
The barber tries, as oft before
To make my thinning locks look more,
Yet nothing hides the balding patch -
It's an empty barn that needs no thatch.
Thank you so much, I'd love a nut
To crack between my molars, but
My dental plate won't stand the shock.
A custard tart to it's a rock.
  Yet now the pace of life suits me.
  Less rush, more time to stand and stare,
  To jog the failing memory
  Be grateful for the love and care.
  Time to recall the happy years,
  Time to forget those futile tears.
  Time to set the house in order
  Before the call 'across the border'.

    Old age, lost youth? One day you'll find
    That age is only in the mind.

Connie Marsh

Daydreams

An old man, in a dry month, waiting for rain
Dreamed of wetter days and his lost youth
When fields were green and rivers ran
And the sap was rising, and desire
A flame, flared in answer to flashing eyes
Then steadied and burnt bright, for many years.

His longing now, like the parched grass here
Feared that spark, that might uncontrolled, return
Leaping from grass, to leaf, to bough,
Consuming tired flesh, dry joints, and aching limbs
Or would it, like youth's elixir, free him from pain,
Refresh and renew, or just bring more tears.

Geoff Hockley

7 Ages Of Man

It all begins with the earth and the wind,
Moving as one, let the rains in,
Creation makes life, a new miracle found,
A trickle of water springs from the ground.
Soon it becomes a bubbling brook,
Laughing along the pathway it took,
It sends fallen twigs spinning in swirls,
Splishing along its safe woodland world,
All of a sudden, the brook is a stream,
It doesn't know where it is going,
Of care where it's been.
It fights undercurrents and feels so alone,
With no sense of direction, it wants to go home.
But life keeps it moving, with loving devotion,
Time takes it along, until it's an ocean,
Part of so many streams, who now lap as one,
Relaxed now and settled its growing is done.
Years pass by slowly, the seas overflow,
It know it is time to move on, to go.
It joins several others, who choose the same way,
Now gentle rivers, they flow away,
They ripple along, slower and older,
Their waters are shallow, darker and colder,
Their time in this world is over, they know,
So they're taken to heaven, to the rain clouds they go.
Showering water all over the earth
Joining fresh winds, and inspiring new birth.
And so over fields, and hilltop and plain,
The cycle of life can begin once again.

Angela Dawson

Disused Airfield

Here cattle crop the grass
And straggling weeds have grown
Between some granite blocks
Of broken stone
And here a hanger derelict
From weather and neglect
Has fallen down
The runway just a rough brown
Line across this open space
An ever-poignant sign
That here in this deserted place
Heroic deeds were done
And in the sighing wind I hear
A spitfire's engine roar
And see those youthful ghosts appear
On this forgotten airfield where
They cheerfully waved a last farewell
Then fought their final war.

Jessica Frank

Deception

The inner reaches of the power house,
The deeper realms of the sanctum unexplored,
Within these depths, a web of thoughts unchallenged
Seek endlessly to lurk lest they be bared
To those who could interpret any sign,
And start to scratch on tissues ever clear
The word that's sharply spoken to deceive;
To lay a trail from thoughts ere they be seized,
And lead the knowing to the very edge;
Too easy were it could we simply speak
Of what we hold beyond, just out of sight,
Yet trusting to be found in fruitless labour;
So smash the bonds that grip you to this mask
Unfold that cloak, before this night be past.

Molc

INNOCENCE LOST

The wind some higher voice obeyed;
Peace in the thrushes' nest betrayed;
Ran restless over every roof,
Howled and galloped upon the hoof.
Sudden spiral churnings of leaves
Formed russet harlequins beneath the eaves
Possessed but for the moment's dance;
The solitary ballet of Providence.

Idle, lame tree bones cracked;
Sabred clandestine claws raked
The song-borne leaves, autumn's mosaic,
While skeletal trees in the swell, frantic
Heaved as though the next refrain
Would from the earth extract their train
Of clay-fronded tendril, adventurous root;
Put to cold sleep this arboreal moot.

Out on the wind-blown field
Stood statuesque, epic, an old man who did yield
As an old wise tree, to this firmament;
At peace, he - head bowed to the inclement
Subjugating wave bittering the blood;
Ponderous, stock-still, as if his eighty-five
winters could
Abate the lust of the youthful wind -
He knew better than to in anger raise his hand

Against her livid wheeling,
And so stood in acquiescence, while the reeling
Of winter song, fieldward-cast ravens
Indignantly coughed from their woodland havens -
No match, he was, he knew
'Gainst those winds that indifferent blew;
Saw in octogenarian wisdom the truth
That he had battled fruitless with these winds,
in his innocent youth.

Seán Rooney

To Tom

Master why? When? Where and How?
Why do they call it the Houses of Parliament
when it as big as a palace?
Why do they have all those green seats?
Daddy says 'It is where MPs sleep.'

Why do you sigh
When I ask, why did Granny die?
Daddy says 'She is up in the sky'
What is it like dying?
Last night I dreamt I was flying
I flew right up into the sky
But I didn't see Granny.
Maybe she is a star.
I didn't fly that far.
How were the stars made?
Daddy says there was a big bang.
'Did you hear it Grandad?'
Mummy says 'There is a man on the moon.'
I bet his mummy hopes he will come home soon.

Jack Major

CAESAR

The clock's moon-face
Swallowed another minute
And announced your birth-time
7.52 (as the rush-hour trains swelled).
Yanked from my split belly you must have gulped
Your first piece of jagged air.
A shrivelled plum, your alarm
Rang sexless through two rooms
To your father.

At 7:53 they must have cut our cord
The food chain, your pulsating path
Back to the old world. Clipped and tagged
Like a screaming bird, the cold scales
Welcomed your arrival, measured your wholeness.
As I lay in enforced oblivion (my spirit somewhere
Grateful of relief) the bikini wound was
Mopped and mended as if in apology:
Your birthmark.

Empty of your gentle kicks
At 8:15, unburdened and unbloody, I was taken
Half-awake to where you were, now
Sexed and swaddled in your father's arms
A small blue question mark, your face
Searching for the milky smell of love.
But I slipped away again before I held you
And hours lost themselves
Before we met.

Catherine Rose

THIRD WORLD

I see
Your life of
Death and destruction
Your desolate faces.

I hear
Whistling shells
Distant explosions
Your anguished cries.

I smell
Rotting corpses
Blazing homes
Your terror.

I taste
The despair
Of your suffering,
Your gall.

I touch
A button
And adjust
My senses.

Rosaline Pilley

CHANGING DIRECTIONS

I remember when
Monday mornings made me wince,
The daily grind would re-commence
And traffic jams become the norm
As into work again I'd storm.
No time to read or please myself
My hours are filled by work - what else?
I lived for Friday afternoon
It really couldn't come too soon;
But Saturdays and Sundays too
Were filled with chores I couldn't do
Throughout the week when I was working;
What I'd give for a bit of shirking
Then came the magic day last summer
Decided I would do a runner.
An offer too good to be true
Retirement! Now what shall I do?
I felt my answer must be yes
It surely would be for the best
So grabbing back my life with glee
I find I've lots of time for *me!*

Wendy Brennan

THE STREAM OF LIFE

A silver jet spurts forth
From Mother Earth,
Trickling tentatively
O'er her vast bosom.
A babe is born.

Joyously skipping,
Frisking, dancing
Over glistening pebbles
Gathering momentum.
A child is growing.

Exploring, thrusting
Down slippery slopes,
Round rocky crags,
Exulting in strength
and force.
A youth is formed.

In turbulent torrents,
Precipitous falls,
Swirling and thundering
On a dangerous course.
A man comes forth.

Meandering gently,
Its force now spent,
Placidly wending
A calm way to the sea.
Old age has come

Almost imperceptibly
It slips into the sea:
Its turbulent course
Might never have been,
Man is swallowed up
in *death!*

Monica O'Sullivan

ANY TIME SOON

In warmth of life
I sense a death
Rise up, take flight
A final breath.
Cold fingers twist
And ice your heart,
Do not resist
The journey's start.
On golden wing
To soar through light,
May sunset bring
My final night.
And with it peace
My heart to fill,
This sweet release
My world be still.

Paula Cooper

MAN

His life evolved from grains of sand
But always wanting more,
He sold off all his promised land
And had less than before.

His threads of life had come apart
And no-one really cared,
But hidden deep within his heart
His wild dreams were still there.

Now television, radio
Feeds him up on lies,
But he who turns away from that
Will in the end be wise.

Poisons, poppies, sometimes weed,
He plucks, and wastes away,
Yearning things he does not need,
He breaks and robs and slays.

Tarra Eve Flint

Who Am I?

Who am I, that was hushed aside, yet was called back by Jesus,
with arms opened wide.
Who am I, that sees with eyes clear and bright, with innocence,
with honesty,
So meek, oh so mild, who am I? I am a child.

Who am I, that's growing so fast, I am actually behaving like
others at last.
Who am I, that's forgetting to see with innocence, with honesty.
Who am I, that starts to reason why, trying good and bad,
Who am I, that now cares nothing, for what I was, or what I had.

Who am I now, that life's moved on, who am I now, it's almost gone.
Thinking back, my mind grows clearer, now honesty is moving nearer,
Now I am thinking how safe, how secure I felt,
When I was oh so meek, oh so mild, when I was just a little child.

Who am I now, the years all filed away in God's great book,
Seems now I know why Jesus looked at me, and smiled,
You see, I am still just His helpless child.

Oh yes, though fully grown and filled with years,
With foolish doubts, and oh so many fears,
I hear a voice call to me from whence I came,
I hear a voice calling me by my name, now I push my fears aside
And am called back by Jesus, with arms open wide.

Who am I that can again see, with inner joy, with honesty,
Who am I, that can feel again, His love, so meek, oh so mild,
Yes. it's me Lord, I am coming home, *for I am, your child.*

Paula Penfold

LIBERATION

Once upon a time there was a little girl
Who, at an early age, was thrust into the world.
All sorts of things came to her, all of which she understood
She learnt that to survive, she might not be too good.
Through each new day, week, month and year the world
became her school.
She travelled through her sordid life but, was not taken for a fool.
She was taking a rollercoaster ride and savoured every peak
And with each new encounter made her strong, not weak.

Two years into her teens she discovered to her relief
An acute sensation of a hidden, deep belief.
A purity of indulgence and a freedom of her soul,
An openness to all who served her without losing control.
Upon her life's experience she entranced and entwined
With each spell that she cast and the powers of her mind.
She performed her carnal rights with each new curtain call
And always thought to herself no-one will see me fall.

She entered double figures before her twenties, I'm afraid.
Living for revolution. With herself a pact was made.
She became a mistress of disguise - ever-changing, something new -
To touch the hearts of all she met. You'd know if she touched you.
What happened to this little girl, how does this story end?
In sweet fairytale fashion I ask you my dear friend?
She brought with her a language and taught a new generation.
Now all who speak in her tongue speak only of liberation.

Deborah Ellis

THE STAGE OF LIFE

Wise men call us players
Upon the stage of life,
Acting out our destiny
Amid the toil and strife.

Afraid to show our feelings
All weakness we must hide,
Blinded by our ego
Masked by foolish pride.

As the pages slowly turn
Let our light shine through,
Show concern and modesty
To ourselves be true.

Our stay on earth is only brief
But watch the play unfold,
It's up to us to set the scene
Make each moment gold.

The world would be a better place
If people all would try,
To drop the cloak of falsehood
And cease to live a lie.

B G Harwood

STROKE VICTIM

Come be my love
Let's through the years
Travel rejoicingly together.
We did, we did!
Careless of time
So much to do, so many tastes to savour
Certain of more tomorrows
Life seemed so full.
I watch you now
Gaunt and with haunted eyes
Lost in a frightening world
Peopled with broken images.
I hold your hand
There's nothing left to share.

Joanne Taylor

WHEN YOU CAN HEAR THE ANGELS

(After R Kipling's - 'If')

When you can hear the angels call above you,
You may spurn them, if you so choose to do;
When you can see that only Death pursues you,
And resents you, you may resent It too;
When you can't sleep - or cannot keep from sleeping,
You may - on waking - drive your heirs away,
Or when weeping - you may soon stem the weeping,
And lure a few - the favoured few - to stay.

When you are cheered - you star in your own drama;
When you are roused - you play the despot's part;
You may not learn the nature of your Karma,
But this is Eld; the last performing art,
And though you rue the loss of once fine features
Long ravaged by the dark realms of the mind,
You need not sigh with this land's ancient creatures,
Who are like you - but are the meeker kind.

When you can feel too many days were fashioned,
On deeds undone; on songs unwisely sung,
You may rise up with your bold heart impassioned,
And tease Fate with the barbed wit of your tongue,
And you can goad those past dreams into actions,
With new-found power of spirit and resolve,
And need not envy Youth, nor all its factions,
Which will one day diminish, then dissolve.

When you can face the fading years with relish,
Although your peers concede like broken mules,
Where'er they lie, they soon will quietly perish,
While you employ your nous to flout the rules,
And He who pens the last line of your sonnet,
Condemns you as you writhe against the trend,
But this cruel Earth - and every soul upon it,
Applauds you to a hero's end, dear friend!

Anna Petherick

It's All Downhill From Here

When your memory has faded
And your privacy is invaded
By the sound of modern music in your ear,
When your hair is getting thin
And your teeth just won't stay in
Then it's all downhill from here.

When you need a stick for walking
And you do a lot of talking
To yourself; because there's no-one to hear,
When you can't control your ills
Despite an hourly dose of pills
Then it's all downhill from here.

When your muscles are all flabby
And you're always feeling crabby
And you've got a hearing aid behind your ear,
When your eyes have lost their twinkle
And you cannot find your winkle
Then it's all downhill from here.

When you've made your peace with God
And your head begins to nod
And death's no longer something that you fear,
You don't want to live much longer
For the pains are getting stronger
And it's all downhill from here.

David R Williams

TO TEENAGE GIRLS IN THE 1990S

(Apologies To Rudyard Kipling)

If you can keep your maidenhead when all about
Are losing theirs and making fun of you.
If you can trust yourself when all men pressure you
If you can wait and not be tired of waiting
Or being lied about, to heck with lies;
Or being blackmailed. Don't give way to blackmail;
And yet don't look too good or sound too wise.
If you can force your heart and nerve and sinew
To fight them off till all your strength is gone;
And so hold out till there is nothing in you
Except the will which says to them 'Hold on!'
If you can dance all night and keep your virtue,
Flatter the posers, keep the common touch;
If neither nerds or yuppie geeks can hurt you
If all men count with you but none too much.
If you escape the clutches of a chauvinist
With sixty seconds' worth of distance clear
Yours is the power and possibly the glory
And what is more, you won't get AIDS my dear.

Elisabeth Berreen

The Ages of Eve

What's in a baby girl's smile,
What's in a baby girl's smile?
    A million kisses, a million tears,
    A million hopes and a million fears,
What's in a baby girl's smile?

What's in a little girl's smile,
What's in a little girl's smile?
    With sparkling eyes and dimpled chin,
    She'll steal your heart and take you in,
What's in a little girl's smile?

What's in a schoolgirl's smile.
What's in a schoolgirl's smile?
    Laid aside the dolls and toys,
    Because she has discovered boys,
What's in a schoolgirl's smile?

What's in a maiden's smile,
What's in a maiden's smile?
    Her diffidence is laced with art,
    Sweet innocence with Cupid's dart,
What's in a maiden's smile?

What's in a woman's smile,
What's in a woman's smile?
    Soft promises your heart to spur,
    And bind 'til you belong to her,
What's in a woman's smile?

What's in a matron's smile,
What's in a matron's smile?
    Surface charm and sweet content,
    Mask menopausal male torment,
What's in a matron's smile?

What's in an old crone's smile,
What's in an old crone's smile?
    Her eyes have seen it all before,
    Her chatter is an awful bore,
    That makes you welcome death's dark door,
What's in an old crone's smile?

P E A Richardson

Too Old At Forty-Nine

Along the street, a man comes shambling homewards,
Bowed and beaten, old before his time,
Long miles he's walked today, and hardly eaten,
No work, no work, is all he's heard them say,
Another day has gone in fruitless searching,
He knows he'll never work again,
Too old. Too old for everything,
Too old, and looks it. Too old at forty-nine,
Tomorrow he will walk the streets again,
Hopelessly, despairingly, he'll try,
Maybe just this once, there will be something,
There's nothing else to do, he must go on,
To try again, again. Does no-one care,
How shameful, how heartbreaking,
To be too old! Too old at forty-nine.

Ivy Garriock

Untitled

the little girl from childhood
wanted only to be loved
a warm caress, a father's hand
someone who understood

the little girl in shadows
with a heart as large as day
wanting only to be cared for
and to give her love away

the little girl in twilight
with the darkness near at hand
reaching out in fear and trembling
is there someone there? a friend

the little girl in darkness
all her life the coldness rings
the only thing she's asked for
that life can never bring

and in the wind I hear her
in the sea I feel her pain
she haunts me from the past
and lives with me again

the little girl, a woman now
her heart upon her sleeve
the pain of never being loved
to this she can't concede.

Susie Barker

To Anodene Urenia Smith

I came across a bookmark
in an old, old book -
an Arthur Rackham lady
in gorgeous Persian silks -
and on the other side
in familiar script was scrawled
'Anodene Urenia Smith'.
I wrote that name once,
on a schoolgirl whim,
but I cannot remember
the she that I was then -
cannot re-enter her mind
And she could not imagine
the things that I now know
(thank God),
or feel what I have since felt.
She had the world once,
limitless at her feet -
uncharted, undefined.

B Allen

WHAT IS LIFE

We start out as a tiny seed getting all the food we need
Growing in a confined space, until the world we have to face
Screaming as we gasp for air, into our mothers' loving care
Nurtured through the tender years, allaying all the new found fears.

Our childhood memories soon fade when adolescent plans are made
Being young and so naïve, doing things that we believe
Disagreements moody faces, we put our parents' through their paces
Growing up we're so confused, our elders sometimes not amused.

It's time for us to leave the nest, our parents having done their best
We have a partner of our own, it's now our turn to build a home
Creating life and all it means, fulfilling all our hopes and dreams
Forward do we have to lead, teaching children of our seed.

Tables turned it's them and us, understanding all the fuss
From our parents' generation, of their rules and regulations
We look at it with reservation, as illness strikes our preservation
Time to put our life in order, with this cancerous marauder.

Shedding tears of frustration, with this travelling mutation
How intertwined our lives have been, nothing that I would redeem
I have to go, I feel at peace, my beating heart will gently cease
I cannot start my life anew, but I'll be watching over you.

Bernice Meechan

YOUTH

I think of my youth,
when I look at my son,
and think of the crazy things that went on.

Gangs in the street,
Learning to smoke,
Fashions to follow,
Drinking coke.

Twenty five years on,
I wonder where the time has gone,
Mistakes were made along the way,
Tears and laughter on each day.

My baby girl plays,
she has no cares,
The problems of the world, she's unaware.

When she's a teen,
with much different ways,
We'll tell her of our teenage days.

She'll laugh and cry,
Life's cycle goes on,
and she'll wonder where
the years have gone!

Christine Miller

D Day

It was, for some, their 'shining hour' which nothing can ever equal.
Before that event was the 'preliminary' and after was just the 'sequel'.
The few hectic months of preparation for war before that day in
September when 'our world ended' was a time that only 'we few'
can remember.
Now that time is history and recounting those days is a bore.
Trying to relive our past - forgetting the terror that petrified our core
and 'stiffened our sinews'. The tedium whilst paper was shuffled by
bureaucracy
We were used like cards in a gambler's game; destined to save
democracy!
Who would live to tell the tale of the lives with which bureaucracy had
gambled and about the men who were landed in France; across the
beaches they stumbled.
For the ones who were landed first there's an inalienable right to bore.
They were there! They struggled on and watched as the bullets tore
their friends to pieces - death is not always a sweet release.
There is sometimes screaming agony before that final peace.
Do we do a disservice by giving to that time such a patina of glamour
disregarding the filth and blood, the betrayal and mind numbing
clamour?
Memory is selective and not capable of truthful accounting
When the discussion gets heated and the tension is mounting,
one way to stop the stories of these men and their very real daring
and to save them from the humiliation of discovering that no-one now
is caring.
I just have to say one sentence to stop them in their tracks.
'When I landed on the beach in France' - because I'm a woman it lacks
quite the impact it should have. Males simply don't want to know
that women really did take a small part in that undeniably male show.
No-one wants to demean them nor diminish what they bravely achieved
but including women in their macho tales - it's not to be believed.

They don't want to hear it I'm convinced that it cannot be just chance
that when a woman says 'I was there' and tells of the circumstance
their memory inexplicably lapses and suddenly the glory
has dwindled.
Interest unaccountably dies and cannot be re-kindled.

F O'Brien

FAST CARS AND BUXTON CHAIRS

I wish I'd known you long ago
when rebels bobbed their hair,
The cars you travelled in were fast,
before the Buxton chair.

Your sepia prints are filled with friends.
Bees gathering round the honey.
In those sweet years the world was yours,
For you had wit and money.

Back in the days when you had teeth,
you wore a dazzling smile.
You effervesced with social grace,
and all you did had style.

But social charm and wit and smiles
were thickly painted on,
over a deeper lonely self.
Now all that paint has gone.

So when you laugh, your heart joins in
and now you don't pretend
you know us, for you love us all,
and everyone's your friend.

Marian Griffin

MATURITY

Feeling.

Needing loving.

Wanting.

Growing.

Desiring.

To be desired.

Looking.

Comparing.

Crying.

Sighing.

Sometimes dying.

Unknowing.

Needing knowledge.

Advising.

But in need of advice.

Daring.

Caring.

Dating.

Faking.

Growing up is all these.

And much more.

G J McLaren

PAST AND PRESENT

The sun is shining quite brightly,
upon Mrs Meadows young face.
While Mr Smith and his godson,
are playing a game of chase.

Agnes is talking to mother,
about improving her shop.
While farmer Thomas is thinking,
of ways that will increase the crop.

Molly steps down from the carriage,
and her friends gather round to see.
For today she is going to be married.
What will the future be?

. . . .

Mrs Meadows is watching the telly,
although she's as blind as a bat.
While poor Mr Smith is stroking,
a child's toy of a stuffed cat.

Agnes is trying to cook a meal,
for her mother who died long ago.
While Thomas just makes you feel tired,
as he constantly walks to and fro.

And although she's unable to move at all,
Molly still knows who she is.
Who would have thought in those long ago days,
it would end up being like this.

Jacquie Dimmer

Age Of Confusion

Do not forget me although I have forgotten you all.
Do not dismiss as meaningless and lost the love we once shared.
Love that I can no longer recall.
Whether love in partnership, love in blood relationship or
love in friendship, these different loves we shared were real
and made a real difference to living. They cannot die, although
they are lost in me. Please remember these things. Talk of
them and make them live, although, I have little capacity
for reminiscence.

Do not think badly of me for I realise that I have done these
things to you. But I did not do them wilfully. I did them
because I had to leave, a departure that I had little say in
and one that was premature for me.

When I was able, I loved and remembered you all.

C I Gary Smith

THE MASTERS

We thought we were the masters.
Because we had two legs,
we looked down on four.
Because we could feel,
we thought our feelings mattered.
Because we could think,
we thought we knew it all.
In intelligence,
man was always the most blessed.
Yet possession does not guarantee
use or wisdom.
The Greeks had a word for it:
'Know yourself.'
We are not Gods,
however hard we try.
We thought we were the masters
and died
because we were wrong.

Jennifer Tuckett

The Spirit Of Stories

With fire in one hand and stone in the other
you pleaded with your gods to bring you the next day.
With berries and songs you thanked the animals
for falling upon your spears.
It didn't take long before you snatched and divided the earth.
The animals became slaves and the spirits became bored.
In their different guises they would frighten your stock
and steal away the fair to their fairy folk land.
You invented mechanical slaves to go into the mills.
the spirits reinvented themselves. To grab the attention
the succubus would sit on a man's chest, pinning
him down. Paralysed, his seed would be stolen.
Soon everyone wanted to be seen as the eminent scientist.
You wanted to explain the world around you (to those who knew better)
And still the spirits remained, taking the forms of the past.
(Even the phantasm had to be detected, dissected and explained)
Having packaged and pigeon-holed your surrounds,
you ventured further -
daring to suggest the Divine had little to do with nature.
Hearing tales of abominable creatures roaming forest floor
and sea bed. Truth? Or more products of uneducated,
overactive minds?
Then your thoughts turned to destruction on every level.
And *they* took to the skies, during the day then at night -
daylight discs and anomalous lights. The papers full
of a downed disc, that in the flick of a page became a balloon.
Now you can communicate with your brother on the other side
of the globe, in the tap of a button, and still the spirits stay.
And still they take you; steal your seed and tag you.
If you stay silent you suffer, if you speak out you're ridiculed.

We look forward to stepping from your story to your reality.
See you soon.

B K Toop

THE TRUTH OF OURSELVES

Questions left unanswered from our youth
Our wondering thoughts concealing the truth
Looking back I see a past shrouded in contentment
Misty visions of love and fulfilment
I remember dancing in cornfields with my childhood - my friend
A scene from some old fairytale it lends

The chimes of time though, slowly tick on
And in a blink of an eye that innocence is gone
The magical feeling of finding your life through your games
Discovering your talents, your dreams, your aims
There was a warmth in the depth of my being
The world seemed bigger then, though safe and unthreatening

Questions left unanswered from our youth
Our sensible thoughts concealing the truth
Our truth
The truth of ourselves

Though the magic continues on through time
It changes direction and changes its mind
It crosses borders, finds its own way
Yet close by us it will always stay

Like a childhood friend blossoming with you
Keep faithful and this precious friend will stay true
Stay true to you
For all too soon the dreams will be gone
So fight to keep them alive and keep them strong
And just maybe they might be enough to;

Answer the questions from our youth
Our unleashed thoughts won't conceal the truth
Our truth
The truth of ourselves.

Jane Besser

BRANNY'S BOY

In the early nineteen hundreds I first smelt the mighty Tyne.
They cut my mother open and she gave her life for mine,
and my father joined the herring fleet and left without a sign.
There was no-one left to care for Branny's boy.

The Institute was green and cold, the diet bread and meal,
and the masters used to beat us till our skin would crack and weal.
But we learned to hide our anger and we learned to cheat and steal,
and I learned to take good care of Branny's boy.

By seventeen the yards had called and taken us inside.
As we belted home the rivets, we were fired with heat and pride,
but I stole the coals and timbers and I sold them on the side
for a bit of extra cash for Branny's boy.

And I married bonnie Nellie from the pub on Garston Green
just before her bulging belly brought young Bobby on the scene,
and we settled down to married life though times were pretty lean
and I had to care for more than Branny's boy.

The hunger of the barren years drove most of us to rage
and graduating to the gun I robbed to earn my wage.
Then fifteen years of pent-up hate in Durham's steely cage
broke my soul and made me weep for Branny's boy.

By the time I got the pension I was all alone and frail,
for Nell had died in sixty-five and Bob was in the jail.
He'd followed in my footsteps but I knew that he would fail
for he wouldn't take advice from Branny's boy.

Now in a cheerless room I lie and wait the reaper's drum.
with one-bar heat and stockinged feet I rot inside my slum.
I'll escape from Thatcher's Britain for my time will shortly come
and there won't be many tears for Branny's boy.

Sandy Thomson

ANCESTORS

Mother, father,
Children embraced.
Walk to their daily grind
Where humming Jenny spins
And fingers mend.
Cotton, like snowflakes
Adorns the crowns of the oppressed.

Thus the endeavours
Of Lancashire folk maintain
Their existence.
Backs bend at dawn
And na'er straighten 'til dusk,
Poorly nourished, weary
Bodies falling into beds
Like rows of skittles
Bowled over by the power of industry.

Tiny cogs in a massive wheel,
Pulling straight
The backbone of England.
And in their own tragic, tremendous way
Earning immortality for their generations.

C Ramsden Marshall

SEVEN STAGES

First just a tiny child, a babe new-born
Arising with the sun of life-time's dawn:
Then partial independence of school child;
Life's worries start - peace of home-life defiled.
Childhood moves on, problems of youth set in,
Peace is abandoned for life's strife and din.
Next slightly slower pace, youth left behind,
Dawn of adulthood, better use of mind.
One's children growing, outlook quite mature;
Their hardships, yours, for carefree days a cure!
Step slower, body tired and hair gone grey;
A rocking chair to soothe at close of day.
Till time wins fight and knocks us to the floor.
We land on that - no longer distant - shore.

Olwen France

Last Day

If this were the last day
        of my life
I wouldn't necessarily
        know it
I wonder
if I knew -
what would I do?

I'd probably
        hug and kiss
everyone I'd miss -
that would take up a minute:
I'd surely
        contemplate -
assess my real-estate . . .
reflect upon
the universe
and how
I won't be in it!

S J G

THE PEOPLE'S WAR

Side rival side
Against the tide
Fighting for what
They believe is right
A battle of force
Will run its course
Warmonger see the plight
Suffer and strain
Immeasurable pain
A game of retaliation
Freedom from wars
No more aggressors
Cry the voices of
Every nation.

Karen Jones

THE MEETING -

The sky was blue.
Spring knew no bounds.
The path home seemed long and lonely.
Then, without warning, and eager of step,
You approached, smiling.
With an intensity, our eyes met, our arms entwined;
Hearts, emotion filled, beat at an unfamiliar pace,
faster, faster -
This cannot last.
Then, with the same suddenness that marked your arrival,
you were gone.
Life would never be the same again.
With a heavy heart I walked, without purpose;
the greying sky heralding, out of time, my winter.
You stole my bag
and I feel very, very old.

Helen Harlow

ARTHRITIS

No one knows with arthritis
When it is going to strike
The old, the young, the world over
It crops up where it likes

It doesn't get an invitation
To come and invade our bones
Our joints become stiff and painful
And they creak and grind and moan

Our movements become slower
Our joints get inflamed and warm
Sometimes the pain is so bad
It keeps you awake from night till dawn

Simple jobs become major tasks
Restricted movement in all we do
Why can't we just be dreaming
And wake up feeling healthy and new

It's like fighting a losing battle
But don't ever think of giving in
Just try and fight and be positive
That one day you're going to win

If we all lived in a dream world
We'd get someone to just turn a key
And put everything back to normality
Just think how wonderful that would be

But no matter how bad things may seem
One thing I know for sure
There are people throughout the human race
Who are suffering so much more

S King

IMPRINTS

My love for you will stay the same
Till the sea claims the earth once again
In a never-ending lapping tongue
When the earth will return as it began.

The birds will still fly
But no land for to see
Just prints in the sand
That were once you and me.

My body will be ashes
But my spirit will be free
To love you just as madly
Through to eternity.

Jean Marsh

THE PRIME OF LIFE

A boy stood on the western front, staring from his trench.
He might have been an Englishman, a German, even French.
And through the driving rain, he looked out over 'no-man's-land'.
He saw past all the barricades, began to understand.
He felt so ill at ease, it's quite a shock when you discover.
The one they call your enemy, turns out to be your brother.
He'd grown up in a small town, and married the girl next-door.
The call-up papers came and they sent him off to war.
She was six months pregnant, when he last saw her face.
By the time his son was born, he'd disappeared without a trace.

She often reads his letters, even now through tear-filled eyes.
He was only twenty, but his words were very wise.
'Darling, I hope you are well, don't fret, for I'll survive,
I'll come home from this living hell, your love keeps me alive.'
And through the driving rain, the men were ordered to advance.
They ran toward the machine-guns, they never stood a chance.
He felt a searing pain, it was too late to look for cover.
And there he died, face down in mud, a few yards from his brother.
A boy stood on the western front, and walked toward the light.
He left behind a world gone mad, no sanity in sight!

He was in the prime of life.
A home, a son, a lovely wife.
Now lying on some distant shore.
Another soldier of the 'Great War'.

A boy stood on a grassy hill, and ran back to his mother.
She prayed he'd grow up in a world where men don't kill each other.
But now he's just turned twenty, and it's 1939.
He cuts a dash in uniform . . . a young man in his prime.

Roger Carpenter

GETTING OLD

My shelf-life is over and I feel I've gone to seed
Am I really past my 'sell-by' date?
This is one sad day indeed.

I looked in the mirror this morning -
In fact I started to stare -
Because all I could see looking back at me
Was a wrinkled face and a mop of grey hair.

I wanted grow old gracefully -
Not look the mess that I see,
I don't want to be past my 'sell-by' date -
I want to be a young-looking me.

I don't want all these wrinkles - bags under my eyes -
I don't want to have corns and dry skin -
I don't want these lumpy bits of cellulite -
I want to be chic and thin.

I don't want to be the oldest teenager in town -
To be old mutton dressed as lamb,
But age takes its toll and I'm now an old soul -
And must accept that that's what I am.

Getting old is a mid-life crisis or should I say more of a panic?
I religiously plaster on anti-wrinkle creams
And with each year I become more manic.

Is it such a bad stage reaching pensionable age?
Should one gracefully accept getting old?
Perhaps there's something to look forward to?
When you're old you're wiser I'm told.

You also get free prescriptions and bus pass,
And your children have all left home -
With all your grey hairs and the empty chairs
Does getting old also mean being alone?

Gillie Bishop

ENGLAND DIVIDED

The north and south are divided
In England I've heard say
What a dreadful calamity
When people have no pay.

There is no work for the dockers
Most industry's closed down
The mills they are deserted
Where once the wheels turned round

There is a line through England
This island in the sea
Where people worked together
Together with dignity

The southerners grow richer
Each and every day
Their pockets expanding
As they take home their pay

But their mortgages are rising
As the property market booms
The northerners are sliding
More anxiety and gloom.

This sad divided England
Whose men fought two World wars
So people could live a peaceful life
Less trouble at their doors.

V J Brickley

Ode To The Young!

When you are young you do not worry.
You laugh and play games and are happy-go-lucky.
But as you get older you move along
Getting into trouble and doing things wrong.
Until you decide to calm down and marry.
And start a family in which it will carry
You into the second half of life so merry,
Where you can retire and are ever so happy.
Until you realise that you'll never do
Any of the things that you wanted to do.
For no matter how much you hurry,
Your life will still have passed you in a flurry.
So while you are young,
Please make sure you have fun
And do all the things that you wanted to do.
So that you're not left feeling unhappy and blue,
And wishing that you could live life from beginning to end
To do things over just once again!

Sarah Louise Morris

A Bygone Era

Dancing the Charleston was all the rage.
The roaring twenties a frivolous age.
Short-fringed dresses.
Sleek cropped tresses.

Flappers smoked and drank cocktails.
Men were dapper in white tie and tails.
Morals became slack.
But on one looked back.

Flat-chested girls were thought the bee's knees.
Brazenly flirting - loving to tease.
With feathers in headbands.
And pearls in long strands.

A brand new era for bright young things.
Wearing cloche hats and diamond earrings.
All night long played jazz.
Non-stop razzmatazz.

To do the fox-trot was thought risqué.
They only lived to cavort and play.
A fast ride in a car.
'Simply spiffing by far;'

The pace of life was ripping and fast.
But not forever would this fun last.
These were outrageous years.
Sadly later came doubts and fears.

Pam Lewis

ALMOST THE END

The hearse was standing
outside the chapel of rest,
where frosty sunlight
changed the leaded, muted panes.

The driver, waiting,
heard the final hammer blows
cracking the crisp air,
outside the chapel of rest.

The coffin lying
inside the chapel of rest,
where winter sunbeams
lit the polished brass and wood.

Jo Brookes

THE SIXTH AGE

A legacy of my sporting days - a knee complication.
This contrasts my wife, who enriches her life
With Ramblers' walking and 'keep-fit' talking.
My forte is crosswords and navel contemplation.

Unlike her insomnia I sleep like one lost,
I watch sport at weekend, she's off the deep-end.
While her opera cassettes they make for upsets.
We compromise, harmonise, keep peace at all costs!

Fatuity of expectation is somewhat entrained:
I hate to admit it, but facts bespoke fit it.
To coin a phrase, the throes of our days
Are tempered by fate and our end is ordained.

Time was when 'sleep' had deeper meaning:
We'd fantasise ahead, impatient for bed,
We're loath now to say, at the end of the day,
One's sleep's more insistent than 'tweening.

Thoughts of our seventh age are fearsome we grant,
We know it'll come, that we'll both succumb.
Oblivious of striction we'll pass on this dictum:
'Enjoy health while you can, there's many that can't.'

A W MacEwan

UNTITLED

Water
Desert
Flood and tears,
Vanity
Necessity
Over the years.
Coal fires
Forest fires
CFC's,
Present
Future,
No more trees.
Ozone
War zone
Hunger and famine,
No redemption for mankind
if he fails to examine.
Thus water, desert, flood and tears
we'll inherit in not too distant years.

Michelle Francis

SMILER

There's a bright, grinning face mocking me,
blocking my view of the 'picture box',
gloating over my immobility . . .
My feet are too warm from the socks.

I push them off, and enjoy the cool
air between my small wriggling toes . . .
The bulbous creature is still there - I drool,
vexed, determined that 'smiler' *goes.*

Struggling free of heavy, fleecy sheet,
I wriggle down from cotton pillow,
lash out at the leering torture with both feet,
miss, yet catch the string with a toe.

The figure spins, swinging out of reach
but I time it right and kick it true
and again, again - oh, that was a peach,
from cot the hateful bauble flew!

I gurgle with great delight and joy
finally rid of that grotesque 'pain' . . .
then mother's there, fussing over her boy -
soon 'smiler' blocks my view again.

Phoenix Martin

BIRTH

Piercing cry marks the entrance of a new human being,
Kicking and screaming into the concrete confines of the delivery room!
Marking the end of almost ten months of morning sickness,
strange food cravings, hormonal mood swings and bodily changes,
Culminating in the geyser rush of the waters breaking and the regular
contractions of labour pain.
Grabbing the pre-packed suitcase and rushing my wife as swiftly and
gently to the car as possible,
Panic and anxiety mark the angst-ridden trip to the maternity hospital.
Her face now darkens as she concentrates on the task in hand,
Breathing regularly between the contractions, her face twists
and contorts,
Reflecting the culpable inner rage of her body undergoing a
tortuous action!
Wheeled into the delivery room, she grasps my hand in an inhuman
vice-like grip,
Shouting and stating that mother nature is totally unfair in the
creation process!
Beads of perspiration rapidly turn into rivulets with the enormous task
of divorcing two separate beings joined like Siamese twins within the
restrictive enclosure of one body!
Her stirruped legs now move with the rhythmic pelvic motion of
pushing the baby out.
After what seems an eternity, a fluid-endrenched head appears,
followed by arms, torso and legs,
Attached to the lifeline of the glistening umbilical cord.
My mind dazed with this novel experience switches off to what goes
on afterwards,
As the shrieking, cleaned bundle of joy is placed in my arms.
A healthy, normal daughter! Hallelujah! Praise God!

Robin Halder

FALLEN ANGELS

In amongst the flames I flit
As soul is to flesh
Breathless glassy heat
Unbearable
Yet born and born and born

Very dust jumps at my touch
As will is to deed
Tumbled puppets rise
Unwilling
To dance and dance and dance

I am of no matter
But without it cannot be
Nameless seeker strive
Unrelenting
And wake and wake and wake

Light will slip your weighty flesh
Chains will drop away
Squinting family fly
Unceasing
Come home come home

Come home

Jose Lacey

The Seed

At first a seed does not exist
It is not allowed
In the world
Then suddenly
One day
It becomes a substance
It is capable of existence
The seed is nursed
It cries out and is comforted
It smiles sweetly at the world
As every day it grows
More aware
Over the days
Its smile disappears
It begins to fear
Its daily existence
It is polluted by the foul air
It cannot breathe
And is stifled and sheds a tear
Men and machines
In the atmosphere
Destruction and decay
Everywhere
The seed begins to fall
Slowly it fades
Below the line of destruction
It withers away
And the seed dies.

Mary Mullett

CREMATED EQUAL

All men are created equal;
Until careful conditioning
By well-meaning parents,
Preachers, friends and teachers,
Breeds bigotry into innocence,
Equality can only be restored
By six feet of earth
And a wooden box.

David Atkinson

QUIET THOUGHTS

One remembers; can one forget
Those days gone by and somehow yet
How can these memories be forgot;
So should we let them go, or not?

To sit and dream, while memories linger;
Tracing gently with mental finger,
One remembers those childhood days,
Days of pleasure and love always.

Times remembered through various ages;
Learning to live in all life's stages;
A battle won, a lesson learned,
Sometimes encouraged, sometimes spurned.

Remembering too, times that were dark,
That left behind an indelible mark;
Of friends, companions, or a date,
That we cannot eradicate.

Memories recent; memories sublime;
Something to remember all the time;
As life goes by, we dream still more;
Who knows what in our mind we'll store?

One remembers; can one forget
Those days gone by and somehow yet
How can these memories be forgot,
So should we let them go, or not?

H Val Horsfall

IN THE BEGINNING!

It all starts when you arrive, here on planet Earth,
The product of a formula, known as giving birth,
They grab you by the ankles, and you are taken aback,
The innocent party in the room, you're the one they smack.

Now everyone is happy, because they have made you cry,
Then at your little bits and pieces, they now start to pry,
Every meal you get is milk, if you drink it they are happy,
It is not so when in the night, you unload it in your nappy.

The things they tried to tell us when we were little kids,
We used to sit and listen, thinking they had flipped their lids,
Well when you think about it, could a cow jump over the moon,
And then there was that randy dish, who ran off with a spoon.

They said the owl and the pussy cat, put to sea in a pea green boat,
Believe that if you like, but that cat would have had him by the throat.
What about that Humpty Dumpty chap, he had a very nasty fall,
They don't tell you how that big thing, first got up on the wall.

After learning our nursery rhymes, we now go outside and play,
Then it's unbelievable, when you hear what your parents say,
They watch you while you play, but shout when you climb a tree,
'If you fall down and break your leg, don't come running to me.'

Sometimes when they call you, their shouts fill you with fear,
Hysterically telling you, 'I'll wring your neck when you get here.'
Now with the threat of GBH you are thinking, what shall I do,
But in the end you go to them, as you know they still love you.

Wenn The Penn

NEIGHBOURHOOD WATCH

Streets are always highly interesting places,
'Cause living there are many different faces.

Ordinary households and some that are odd,
Rowdy yobs and people who worship a God.

The brother and sister who argue and fight,
All through the day and most of the night.

Single mothers with loads of kids,
Too many children and not enough quids!

Young families just starting out,
With dreaded mother-in-laws lurking about!

The bespectacled professional couple,
Who would never be the cause of a scuffle!

Vehicles can tell us a lot,
About the money these people have got.

There's the foul-mouthed teenage rocker,
The studs, rings and chains are a shocker!

And we mustn't forget the 'little old dear',
The oldest resident who has always been here!

A colourful spectrum of people's lives,
Showing through a mixture of vibes.

C Shadwell

SEA-LIFE

Sirens wading through oil filed beaches,
Seagulls scream out their death-dives,
Crabs shrink into rainbow coloured sand,
Capitalists laugh at their bank account dreams,
Whilst urchins cry out for loose change
to relieve another cardboard dream.

Sea horses parley for fares
from drunken amoebas whilst they split into schizophrenic parodies.
And sharks pedal barbiturates
to innocent and juvenile seal pups.
Cod herd themselves into 9-5 nets
to be taken to an early grave or diner's plate
battered and abused; looking sky bound through glazed eyes.

Dolphins cackle at tuna whilst hazily sitting in blue seas;
screaming road rage at trawlers
and suffocate whilst caught by the net labelled stinger,
To end up as flat breathless scraps for lobsters to salvage
and take back to their hovels from which they call home.

Jason S Breed

TWO FACES

She was always more popular
I don't know why:
Selfish, pig-headed and dirty
I was just shy.
Everyone loved her because she was different,
but I knew her.
She was horrible to me, cruel you could say,
That's the way things were.

Claustrophobia set in; as did a new low.
Once my best friend, now my ultimate foe.
But what could I do?
Oh, if only I could send a sign or show
how little she cared for them (or anyone else)
I would be happy - but that would be cruel.
I am a fond fool -
That's the way I am . . .

She is still more popular
I still don't know why.
She's still selfish, pig-headed and dirty,
And I am still shy.
But one thing is certain
though I tried to make them see,
Her character is a curtain,
And that's the way it will be.

Ashley Campbell

Growing Up

She used to be a happy babe
She'd chuckle all day and smile
She learned to talk so quickly
Took just a little while
She used to be a chubby girl
When she was just a child
Then she grew into her teenage years
And became a little wild
Each week she'd try something new
Clothes or a food fad
I'd feel for her if she was down
I didn't want her sad
She grew into a young adult
Sensible pretty and fun
I'd like to think it's because of me
You see I am her mum.

Joy Benford

Sleep, Come Quickly

The plea

Sleep, come quickly
I need you to descend upon me
to close my eyes,
make steady my breathing,
and my heart beats too slow.

My body cries out to you!

I love you sleep. I would weep did I not love you.

The arrival

But as sleep's warm promise closes my eyes,
calms my body, steadies my breathing, slows my heartbeats,
and makes my limbs heavy and my body tingle,

The memory

I remember my grandmother.

A numb emptiness is in my stomach

The feeling

grief

sleep
I think

will not come now
quite
so quickly.

E Clarke

Reluctant Hero

(For the centenary of Wilfred Owen, War Poet)

He never wanted to be a soldier,
Didn't dream he would go to war,
He imagined he'd be like his father,
Sail the seas, see the lands he saw.

He never wanted to be a hero,
Didn't dream he would kill those men,
He imagined a foreign foe,
'Shoot to kill' merely words till then.

He never wanted the shame or glory,
Didn't dream he could feel so cold,
He imagined the media story,
Then shot himself, eighteen years old.

Betty Lightfoot

In The Forest Of The Mind

I am a tree, rotting, decaying,
My leaves are trodden and trampled under foot,
My bark is carved and scarred with initials,
Inflicted by humans with penknives.
I am a tree out of my tree,
Bats in my belfry,
Depression in my brain you see,
It's driving me insane mentally,
The blackness, despair and the torment,
Constantly descending on my every waking
And sleeping and conscious hour daily.

Oh, I do so apologise,
Such loss of composure,
Such rantings, such ravings,
Please do forgive.
I rather seem to have quite,
Forgotten myself become quite,
Self-absorbed quite,
Carried away with my thoughts.

But you see,
It wasn't me,
No, not really,
It was the voices,
They do so, so insist,
Upon having their say,
Overpowering and overwhelming,
Like a tree completely riddled,
By the seemly incurable Dutch elm disease,
And oh . . .
How it thrives in a forest!

Denyce Alexander

Upon Reflection

Mirror, mirror, on the wall
Where is that prince, who once stood tall?
Broad shoulders, and a ram-rod spine
Where is that image, that once was mine?

Mirror, mirror, on the wall,
Where is that prince, who once stood tall?
Young Lochinva! who, with, unfailing might,
Would, surely, one day, put the whole world right.

Mirror, mirror, on the wall,
Where is that prince, who once stood tall?
Only you, are left, to know
When? and Why, did he have to go?

Mirror, mirror, on the wall,
Where is that prince, who once stood tall?
Thick, dark, hair, smooth skin and crystal eye
I gaze into you now and can only sigh.

John G McCallion

THE MEANING

By Titan trees,
Whose stately branches decked with shimmering summer leaves
Are lifted gently by the breeze
And then let delicately go
To waver to and fro,
She sits alone and sees
How, by infinitesimal degrees,
The subtly shifting moods
Of morning through to noon,
Of springtime through to fall
Somehow seem to tell her all she needs
To understand what widowhood will mean.

Peter Taylor

THE WATERSHED

It seems, from where I stand today,
My youth running swiftly away
Upon one side, and on the other
Old age gathering up to smother
All that's left into the sea,
The wash and sediment of me,
That little has been done, and think
On rocks no rushing stream could sink:

My old grandfather at his page
Rhyming into his old age
My father's father, tall and stern,
Two children set the soul to learn.
Shall all they worked for, all that gain
Sink down and disappear again
And all those strands just fall apart?
When sometimes it might seem some art
Some wonderful creation might
One day arise and prove them right.

Young, I hated patient thought
What had I to think upon?
Having stolen, found or bought
I must begin a lasting song.

Peter Rist

A Patter to Be Sown

Womb to the cradle, breast to a jar
Life unfolding a future so far
There is a time

Crawling, walking words to be found
Senses responding to visions and sound
There is a time

Questions quite daunting, but honest and true
Thoughts not tainted colour them blue
There is a time

School days to new days, times spent in fun
Winter still sleeping, follow the sun
There is a time

Love, ambitions new paths to take
Time is demanding decisions to make
There is a time

Assessing, guessing time yet to shine
A forgotten paper waiting to sign
There is a time

Yesterday's gone, tomorrow has flown
A pattern completed yet to be sown
There is time.

Terry White

My Son A Man

Now that you have grown older my son
I have advice that I can only give to one
When you step out alone don't be afraid
There will be many a sight to see
So remember all you hear from me

One thing no-one can take away
Is the memory of the day
Always be honest and true
There will be times when you will feel blue
But you will pull through

Try to be gentle and still be firm
Always listen, there's always much to learn
Speak up for yourself, but let others have a turn
Don't ever be afraid to say you are wrong
Don't ever be afraid to say you are right
Always be prepared to fight for right or wrong

Although you may be older my son
Always remember where you come from
I will always love you, you can be sure
And you will always have the love of your Mother pure

When one day you fall in love with another
Don't forget you have a Mother
If a man can not love his Mother
How can he ever love another

Now I know you are able to follow the rules
You can go anywhere with a good set of values
I can feel proud it's true
My son became a man
And that man was you.

Jim Barnes

DEMOLITION

I saw austere walls rise
With a small child's eyes.
My face, cloud won, chilled,
As, down, the wind spilled
Off the vane's sky furrow.
This edifice of toil, built
On the edge of an epoch,
With mortar, as thin
As a post-war dream,
Held firm through the hail
Of every cold war scheme
And the heat of seventy-six.
This year will be its last
And I will bear witness
To the passing,
A mourner or an executioner,
I know not which.
A millennial wind is building
And it has a talon grip,
It's harder and colder
Than nature's worst.
It will dissect,
Remove and re-erect
This family space,
Match this time to place;
New homes for a new age
For those with a digital eye.
I hope they rest easy
In their twenty-first century beds;
I fear they may not, nor I.

Stephen Painting

A

G E

S E X

PYRAMID

Older women, have sagging breasts,
White and wrinkled, fallen crests;
Older men, wear white string vests,
Watch or listen, to cricket tests.

For mature women, sex is an art,
Total pleasure, no stop and start;
Middle-aged men, like brand new cars,
Treating girls, in expensive bars.

Young girls are eager, to go to bed,
But play embarrassed, going red;
Young men just take, what they can get,
Finish up, fed up and frantic.

James Fuller

THEATRE IN THE ROUND

As this old world keeps turning round
We, the characters on the ground,
Here we take whatever life brings
Whether in the limelight or the wings.

We go through life in steps and stages
Turning over the consecutive pages,
Doing the day-to-day performance
All around the clock's circumference.

We move through all the changing scenes
Doleful, hopeful, dreaming one's dreams,
To be a star, to take a bow,
It is there in our make-up somehow.

The comedy, drama, laughter and tears,
The panorama through the years,
So our time does come and go
For life is but a passing show!

The successes and the dismal failure,
The 'props' and all the paraphernalia
Be it joy or be it strife
Such is the backdrop of one's life!

Thus we tread the boards of time
In the real world pantomime,
Playing the king or playing the clown
Till the final curtain is rung down.

Joyce M Atkinson

My Love

Are the summers getting colder?
For winter's chill is in this place,
Or is it we are getting older,
You have that winter look upon your face.
My love.

Once we had our love to keep us warm,
In the open air under a starry sky,
Even through a thunderstorm,
When you thought we might die.
My Love, My Love.

If we still had our strength and vigour,
How the bells would chime,
Then you had a lovely figure,
Do you think we can just one more time?
My Love, My Love, *My Love.*

P M Batch

Back In Time

If I could travel back in time
Arrive before there's clocks to chime
My time machine I'd fully prime
And from the present I'd decline
I'd first see monsters, dinosaurs
Mammoths, sabre-toothed felines,
Volcanoes licking forest floors;
A feral landscape
Back in time

I'd then boost forward to when man
First on this world did walk and climb
A large step in creation's plan
And evolution's last in line
At first they'd have no power of speech
They'd only grunt and move in mime
Then gain the power to learn and teach
In those dark aeons
Back in time

I'd set my controls further still
Emerge in fields as green as lime
I'd see a town perched on a hill
And spires peek over this incline
Great kings and queens have made their stand
From towering castles reign sublime
And peasants melting to the land
Were owned by monarchs
Back in time

Crusading knights sit like machines
On powerful horses swords ashine
And fight whoever contravenes
Their boundaries or their faith's doctrine
They slay for land, they kill for Christ
They rape and plunder, it's a crime
Then they're so proud they've sacrificed
Their blazoned bloodstains
Back in time

I'd then flit forward; leap the lapse
And watch advancement's new design
Industrial age on temporal maps
Man and machine do now combine
Strong steam monsters hiss and puff
Black smoke on landscapes scourged with grime
But for the poor their lives are tough
And nations prospered
Back in time

My next stop, Queen Victoria's reign
The British Empire's rigid spine
Great wealth through suffering and pain
Although this is kept clandestine,
Terraced houses back to back
Face cobbled streets all smeared with slime
While large town houses never lack
A country garden
Back in time

I'd journey on through two world wars
A sight on which my eyes can't dine
But politicians never pause
To turn the world into a shrine
Dictators rise and missiles fall
They must think life's a pantomime
When mushroom clouds, ten miles tall
Destroy whole cities
Back in time

I'd come now to a high tech age
Computers rule and are a sign
That the past has turned a page
For technocrats to want and pine
Unemployment takes its toll
Machines they do the work that I'm
Supposed to do but on the dole
Is where we'll all end up in time

And so the past comes to an end
The present now concludes my rhyme
The future is an unknown trend
And so is travelling
Back in time.

Eddy Shanks

FACTS OF ARMY LIFE

If you join the army
You're surely barmy.

You're sure to lose an arm
Since you won't stay calm.

If you lose your leg
You're bound to lose your head
Then you're really dead.

Those are facts
Of army life.

Melita Colton (10)

The Village Wedding

The bells across the valley ring.
The hymns on wind still faintly sing.
Endless walk to sunlit door,
Beyond who knows we can't be sure.
People smiling, cameras clicking,
Bored young bridesmaid primrose picking.
Cards, speeches, champagne, cake,
Best man wobbly, scrumpy, steak.
Early songs with passion, flare,
Now retarded, bleary stare.
Spongy balloons in groups on the wall,
The turn of the key brings sleep to the hall.
Our bride and our groom some distance now fled,
But poor Mary's mother lies restless in bed.
There are tears on her cheeks;
She mourns daughter gone,
And recalls ambitions she had for so long.
'She'll marry a lawyer, doctor, something like that.'
But she didn't you know; she married a pratt!

Ray Calaz

Ages Of Man

When my children ask
Just how the world began
I begin to tell them
All about ice age
And stone age too
When man became a survivor
Building wooden huts
Making knives with stone, that cut
How this helped him farm
Then came bronze age
Man had found the elements
Man could defend himself
He built forts learned maths and medicine
Fought in wars
With Egyptians, Romans, Saxons
Vikings and Danes
Glittering civilisations with lots of leisure time
Introducing music, games, great arts
But such wars
Over forts and human dominion.

J Dunkley

THAT KNOWING STRANGER

Do I know her?
She seems to think that she knows me
Which of my many previous lives
Has she been a part of?
I think it's not at infant school,
Nor yet the school I attended after that,
She is a part of the adult me,
The which of it is the bit that haunts
As I live through the many places of my life,
The many parts of my life,
The people that I am,
Including the person that I was,
Nursing others, giving birth,
The social round of life,
To which piece does that haunting face belong,
She seems to think that she knows me.

Margaret Boles

LIFE LINE

That newly born baby in the photograph are you sure that was me
No hair or teeth unable to walk or even clearly see
In such a helpless little body I would cry out daily for attention
But in return and in my own way I would always show affection
I'd started on the path in life who knew where it would lead
My family had always been poor and hungry so I chose
wealth and greed
As I fought my way to the top I cared not who I crushed
And the thoughts of normal family life from my mind were pushed
I had made my millions and was considered a successful man
But then one day my heart stopped and I ended up where I began
So in the blinking of an eye my life has passed me by
And as I lie here on my hospital bed I know that I'm to die
This tired old face looking back from the mirror can it really be me
No hair no teeth unable to walk or even clearly see
In my helpless little body I cry out for attention
The nurses are my angels they provide care and affection
I'm nearly at my journey's end but I have a warning I beg you heed
Only loneliness and misery result from power and greed
Life is there for living all too quickly comes the grave
It has no distinction between rich and poor and not one soul
Does it save.

Michael Bellerby

IN MEMORY OF A WELSH TRAGEDY

Imagine if you can a valley of green where all appears tranquil
and serene,
and village life allows children to run free, protected from the ills
of humanity.
Imagine if you can a village school where day begins with
attendance call,
and prayers are spoken with accord, 'For the gift of life we thank
thee Lord.'
Imagine if you can an infant's dream, where riches and adventure
are the theme,
and parents envisage the adult child, their adolescent wars
now reconciled.
Imagine if you can despair so deep where the act of living can make
you weep,
and you survive the passing years trying to stem the shedding tears.
Can you imagine life so surreal where grief is an emotion you
never conceal,
and time running on will never span, the tragedy we know as Aberfan.

D F Baker

STRIVING TO ADULTHOOD

Striving to better our lives
Learning and losing
Innocence lost now
Replaced with experience.

Brutality rules, we learn to protect
Shield and accept
The world's disreputión
Famine and war
Warps our dreams and our fantasies.

Nothing remains
But the terrible truth
Innocence destroyed
Experience conquers.

Helen Knibbs

A CENTURY OF FASHION

In recalling this old century's birth when hemlines
touched the ground in search of deference to modesty,
a well cloaked drape would camouflage the female shape
and trim the bow of apron pert enough to draw a suitor.

But after war and women's vote, the flappers came to vamp
and gloat, with shingled hair and breastless boast
in skirts that daringly displayed suspenders, garters, silken hose
with black for those more prim disposed and proper.

The Thirties threatened further war and coats and dresses
subdued, wore a tailored military look with knee length sense
and shoulders cut and squared for action.
Hair in snoods was highly chic and turbans veiled
the public's view of curlers.

New look in all its elegance defied austerity's abstinence
with swathes of ballerina folds that touched the calf
in classic poise and high heeled dainty shoes
revealed a well seamed nylon ankle.

The Sixties swung in Carnaby Street, the sack gave way
to minis' cheek when girls in boots paraded thighs
and drew both gasps and smiled surprise. Then on to
Flower Power dressing, vibrant sisterhood caressing
self expression, burning bras Eunuch's Greer immortalised.

As the century draws to close with unisex gear and anything goes,
youths with expensive logo longings desire
designer trainers' trappings, whilst shopping malls of
transient fashion reflect the classless denim passion
for Joe Bloggs jeans and Marks and Sparks
a melting pot of self-styled art - unrationed.

Gloria Metcalfe

After Divorce

I feel so unhappy deep down inside
These feelings I try to bury and hide
but they always surface and reappear.
It makes me sad, I want them to disappear
I feel like there is something important missing
I try to explain but no one is listening.
There are tears welling in my eyes
but no one hears my silent cry.
I strive to be strong, have a happy smiling face
but these outward signals mask what I'm feeling inside,
they are so misplaced,
One day I hope to be happy again,
Flourish and be content, be sane,
I long to meet and be with my soul-mate
to share, laugh and grow together,
let it be soon, although it's never too late,
meanwhile I'm holding on and putting my trust in fate.

Elaine Moore

My Life

You passed me on the street the other day,
With your friends you threw rude remarks my way,
'Hurry up Grandad or we'll nick your pension.'
And used some terrible language that I shall not mention.
How old are you? To myself I wonder,
As slowly up the street I plunder.
Eighteen? Nineteen? Just a mere lad,
With no idea of the heartache I'd had,
At the same age as you in the second world war,
For youngsters like you was what I fought for.
These liver spotted hands were once very strong,
And this snowy white hair was once sunny blonde.
My now bent back was as straight as a dye,
And imagine how I felt when I kissed my wife goodbye,
She was four months pregnant with my first child,
And fifteen months later my baby boy died.
I could not be with her to help her with her grief,
And my darling little son, I never got to meet.
So don't mock us oldies, we haven't always been this way,
And when you get to my age, I wonder what you'll say.
Will you have a story to tell? Let's hope it's better than mine.
Or will you be a waster? No appreciating your time,
Or the freedom that you have, the freedom that costs lives.
So just think for a minute, before you shout your jibes.

Wendy Walker

Darling Of The Night

You're a vision on the dance floor
The darling of the night
The men they flock around you
Like moths to candle light

As you gyrate your body
Your skirt rides up your hips
How many young guys watching
Would love to taste your lips

Do you know how much I love you?
Do you know how much I care?
As you erotically move you body
Running your fingers through your hair

When the night has ended
I know you'll be leaving with me
But it doesn't heal my hurting heart
Or these pangs of jealousy

Tell me that you'll always stay
Don't ever set me free
Because I'll be waiting patiently
For the day you dance just for me.

Jennifer Whitehead

THE SEVENTH AGE

'Open wide the door,' he cried, 'and let the fool come in
Who thinks old age and frailty will never capture him;
Who, with his healthy, upright frame and confident demean,
Has not yet known the pain of age, or dreamed what might have been.

Open wide the door, and then remind him that I, too,
Was once admired and cherished by all of those I knew;
I also walked the fragrant earth with arrogance of youth,
But now lie helpless here, embittered victim of the truth.

And once I also held the key that opens every door,
And mocked at death, considering all aged things a bore;
Then years became but moments, and the old and ill were dead,
And horrified, I found that I was old and ill instead.'

Bereft of hope he gazed around with dim and rheumy eye,
Conversing with ghosts from the past, the friends of years gone by;
And as he spoke, his trembling, bird-like hands moved aimlessly,
And reached for things that were no more - things only he could see.

Jo Young

Solitary Reflection

The clock's heartbeat rhythm fills the room,
counting down time on the parking meter of life.
Blurred faces and dyslexic memories, my only souvenirs.
From mother's womb to nature's womb in eighty short years.

Childhood's naiveté and innocence, never treasured, but sadly missed.
Manic hyperactiveness with no purpose, taken for granted,
but now the batteries have run down, the lights dim,
and any form of motion requires careful planning.

A voracious appetite for new experiences and sights,
replaced by a bland, repetitive diet of familiarity.
An ambitious drive for success and its associated trappings,
turned into an imperceptible cul-de-sac of comfortable security.

Raising a family translated into perpetuating the family name.
Lifelong friends that drifted away on a current of apathy.
Years of shared emotions disposed of like spare small change,
where now a five minute visit by a council home help is treasured.

The fresh, inquisitive eyes of inexperience and trust,
have tightened into narrow slits of cynicism and suspicion.
The youth's once half full glass,
now perceived as three quarters empty.

My end of term report card shows,
no questions answered, but many lessons learnt.
Life's learning curve returns to its point of origin.
The circle of life nears completion.

A grain of sand in the desert of mankind,
inconspicuous, I exit life as I entered it . . .
The frailty of a baby's body, wrinkled and vulnerable;
the frailty of an octogenarian, wrinkled and vulnerable.

Kevin Green

REMAINS

Cold,
Bare, bleak,
Charred tanks,
Littered bodies,
Empty shells
Left in chaos.

Sirens pound the chilly air;
While orphans sit restlessly
Sheltered from harm.
Numbed into silence
They enter the light;
The innocent eyes now seen.

Danger has gone.
Destruction takes its place.
A fight for possession.
Triumph over despair.
They kill and get killed.
A celebration of death.

Women look on scattered confusion,
Men have a battle quest.
Weapons pierce,
They do not heal.
More guns? More lives?
Freedom's fight?

Dictators surround a table far away.
Destructive fingers of men
Do not hear or feel
The bombs of terror.
They do not see death,
Only command it.

Claire Louise Jones

Links

The chain I wear around my neck is me
Each link a separate part of my life
Each bead a friend that came and went
Leaving their mark upon my heart
Each joint a place where memories were made
Then left to fade away
As it snaps and falls to the floor
My life begins to turn around
Another love lost and then replaced
Another heart broken then mended
It snaps again
But this time I'm too tired to replace it
So I lay it down to rest
And close my eyes to sleep forever.

Beverley Wilson

Fragile Rope

The guns are silent,
The ammunition lies in
anticipation,
The sky looks down on an
uncertain nation.
This new peace is not yet
seal.
The pain of yesterday war
many still feel.
Blood stained walls,
Gutless buildings.
Reluctant to trust,
Every man is suss.
To some the cease celebration
is in bad taste,
For many their love deceased
now seem a waste.
As victim and perpetrator come
face to face,
For peace initiator this is a
pleasing phase.
The ammunition lies in anticipation
On fragile rope walk this uncertain
nation.

Carol Barrett

WILL HE GO AGAIN TO ENGLAND?

Does he dare go to where
Grey woodsmoke spirals to an ice-blue sky
From frosted hillside farms where sad and listless sheep
Waver their chill lament to echoing air;
In mountain folds and dales the snow drifts deep
Against bare hedgerows and the bones of reeds
Thrust starkly black beside the glassy streams.

Does he dare go to where
Bright daffodils shout their triumph to the host
Of powdered catkins and pale primroses gleam beneath
The leaves, anemones rule before the bluebells
Claim the woodland floor; snakes slough their sheaths
And hedgehogs shrug off saving coverlets
Of undergrowth; birdsong crowds the world.

Does he dare go to where
Sun patterns lace the graceful boughs of beech,
Dance on the fragrant earth, warm-scented after rain,
And laden foxgloves curve their heavy heads
In dappled shade where, time and time again,
The velvet bees plunder their speckled throats
Humming content. A sunlit memory
Delights him and his heart is song.

Does he dare go to where
The soft mist swirls along the river's flow
And rolls across drenched meadows where the rootless trees
Loom darkly, hanging in the cloud-moist haze
Which drifts to no set pattern and he sees
Against the cobwebbed fence, the sheltering barn's
Stone-wet solidity and thus he knows
Home acres; and his heart is tears.

He will not go again to England
He dare not go - suppose it were not so.

Gillian Howarth

EVERY MAN

As a baby you're washed and dressed,
cared for and fed.
As a child you are taught to strive,
to get ahead.
As an adult you work to pay,
for wine and bread.
In middle age your chicks have flown,
don't lead you're led.
In your dotage you're washed and dressed,
cared for and fed.

Barbara Fitzgerald

THE THIEF OF TIME

Out shopping today
Been caught stealing
Glances at the elderly
An old woman in the queue
before me
saw me
And in her reflected gaze
I knew she knew I knew
Each wrinkle tells a story
of some reflected glory
First kiss, first love
Marriage, loss of virginity
Childbirth, death
Sorrow, joy,
World War II
The menopause -
and the wait for the long journey home.

They call us generation 'X' my lot
So I'm wondering when I too am old
and grey, will my wrinkles give me away
Will any wrinkle tell any story?
Will I have visible some reflected glory?

The struggles of the late 20th century
With the Interment, religious cults and men hell bent
on destroying chemically humanity,
The Goddess, the life giver, the weeping mothers of Africa -
When I am out shopping another day?

Tara Feshitan

Seven Ages Of Woman

The early years, when love was all there was
But had no name
For we were only three years old
Innocent as any child.

At twelve we followed love home from school
He pretending not to notice
How we hung on every word and deed
At a distance, no longer children.

Twenty saw the giving of love
That was rejected
We bound our wounds and hardened hearts
For fear of seeming childish.

At twenty-eight a true love grown
Fulfilled in being a couple
Children already at our knee
Who needed our love and were cherished.

At forty odd with work and home
Stretched to our greatest moment
Individual lives so truly found
Yet love continued momentum.

As our young grew up and left
To make their lives their own
We took on even greater tasks
Mature in coming of age.

At fifty plus we stopped to reflect
To know how it had been
Some regrets, some hopes, even dreams
Yet love remains.

Now we know it has a home
That's really all there ever was
Whatever we meet, however life goes,
The child is there, in love.

M Mukherjee

Boy Up A Tree

The breeze with smells of far away
caused leaves to rattle and mast to swoon
On creaking yards the Captain swaggered
high in the heavens above dusty fields.

His ship aimed at the setting sun
which now dripped flames on football ground
where on Saturdays and Boxing Day
the roars of mighty beasts were heard.

And on another ship, a thousand feet below
a mere park bench, in dirty green
two pirates sat with clinking earrings
and painted faces planning deeds unthinkable.

Electric stars above the waves lit up
the path across the Main, and now
with ship hove-to, he scrambled down
limbs scratched, clothes torn, for safety, home and tea.

John Brooks

EVERYMAN

It's been ages. But perhaps . . .
. . . through centuries I have wandered
Knowing life at different points of place
Along the aeons of time
Seen sunlight reflected
Off Roman warriors' armour
Felt the heat off stones
From newly built Greek temples
Or been an urchin poor
On Victorian London streets

Have I loved for a thousand years
Have I battled through
History's brutal landscape
Have I walked with the downtrodden
And hungered in countless generations
Have I been both oppressor and oppressed
And fathered and mothered
Children of the world
Even more than once perhaps
Being parent to my own grandparents.

Who can say? Who can know this everyman?
. . . and yet on a still evening
The mind might brave to ask
Was I was or was I ever will be
And will it ever matter
That knowing this might forfeit
Life's brimming mystery.

Terence E Connolly

INFORMATION

We hope you have enjoyed reading this book - and that you will continue to enjoy it in the coming years.

If you like reading and writing poetry drop us a line, or give us a call, and we'll send you a free information pack.

Write to :-

Poetry Now Information
1-2 Wainman Road
Woodston
Peterborough
PE2 7BU
(01733) 230746